FOR MOLLY:

M U X I M A !

NY, 2.5.08 (52) WITH ADMIRATION +
LOVE ALFREDO JAAR 08

CHILE 1981

BEFORE LEAVING

The journey

Alfredo Jaar left Santiago, Chile for New York in 1981, at the age of twenty-five. His works have been created all over the world, in South America, North America, Africa, Europe, and Asia. He has not had an exhibition in Chile since then; one or two works have been shown, but nothing more. Born in Chile, he left for the first time at the age of five, moving to the island of Martinique with his family. He returned to Santiago in time to complete his secondary education and then to study architecture and film. Shortly after this, he created the project *Studies on Happiness* (1979-1981). And once this was over, he left the country. The story of this departure can be found in the conversations he had in Santiago, in late 2005, with the group that prepared this book (a version of these conversations will be found here, ranging over the whole of the artist's output).

The story that follows, that of his work, is almost too extraordinary to be told. Among other landmarks, he was the first Latin American to be invited to the Venice Biennale Aperto (1986) and to Documenta (the eighth version, held in Kassel in 1987); more recently, his work *Lament of the Images*, shown at Documenta 11 (2002), made an extraordinary impact. He has also participated in the biennials of Sao Paulo, Johannesburg, Sydney, Istanbul, and Kwangju. This year, 2006, he will be at the Brighton and Seville biennials. Works of his have been exhibited throughout the world. He has had individual exhibitions at places such as the New Museum of Contemporary Art in New York, the Whitechapel in London, the Museum of Contemporary Art in Chicago, the Pergamon Museum in Berlin, the Moderna Museet in Stockholm and, most recently, MACRO (Museo Arte Contemporanea) in Rome. His public interventions (starting with *Studies on Happiness* in Chile in 1979-1981) have numbered over forty to date. They have been carried out in places such as New York (Times Square and Spring Street subway station), Washington, San Diego, and Seattle, in the United States; Toronto and Montreal, in Canada; Tijuana, in Mexico; Catia, in Caracas, Venezuela; Rio de Janeiro, in Brazil; Berlin, Frankfurt, Stuttgart, and Leipzig, in Germany; Stockholm, Mälmo, Umea, and Sköghall, in Sweden; Antwerp, Belgium; Lyons, France; Barcelona and Cadiz, Spain; Fukuroi and Niigata, Japan; Kwangju, South Korea; Cape Town, South Africa; and several on the Internet, open to a worldwide public. [1]

Thirty-six monographs have been written about his work. Among the more recent publications, mention may be made of *Emergencia* (MUSAC, Museo de Arte Contemporáneo de Castilla y León), *The Fire This Time: Public Interven-*

tions 1979-2005 (Milan), *Alfredo Jaar* (MACRO, Rome), and *Alfredo Jaar: The Aesthetics of Resistance* (Fondazione Antonio Ratti, Como). He was featured on the cover of publications such as *Artforum* (1990) and, more recently, *Art Monthly* (October 2002) and *Aperture* (winter 2005).

These listings illustrate the extraordinary development of a very contemporary creativity, one that has made Alfredo Jaar a prominent figure on the world scene for the past twenty years and more, as he has maintained and enhanced his position in his three areas of work: public interventions, museums and galleries, and teaching. The artist says that he divides his time equally among the three. His work is not confined to institutional art venues such as galleries and museums; rather, he tries to widen its impact by means of public art interventions and intensive teaching seminars in different academic and community institutions. He is currently a visiting professor at the Center for Public Practice of the San Francisco Art Institute. The honors he has received include the Guggenheim Fellowship (1985); the MacArthur Genius Award from the MacArthur Foundation (2000); and, most recently, the "Premio Extremadura a la Creación 2006" in Spain, a prize awarded to an Iberian or Latin American artist for lifetime achievement, whose jury was chaired by José Saramago, winner of the Nobel Prize for Literature.

Inexplicably, Alfredo Jaar's work was virtually ignored in his own country for many years. For the first two decades at least, international acclaim for his work was paralleled in Chile by a deafening silence, broken only occasionally by articles in the cultural supplements of national newspapers, or by short news items or, recently, by the publication of interviews. Until not long ago, his visits to Chile were for family purposes, although he more than once held conferences where he shared information with students. His notable contribution to the academic seminar on art and politics held in June 2004 by the Consejo Nacional de la Cultura y las Artes, the University of Chile and Universidad Arcis revealed the clamorous enthusiasm of young artists for his work. It also led to a renewed critical interest, once again among people from younger age groups. In 2005 he was at the Faculty of Arts of the University of Chile, directing a workshop where he discussed students' projects. Now, in October 2006, this gradual rapprochement is culminating in his first major exhibition in Santiago, at Fundación Telefónica Chile, and Galería Gabriela Mistral.

The exhibition

Alfredo Jaar's work has barely been seen in Chile since 1981, the exceptions being one piece (*Epílogo*, 1998) in the group exhibition *El final del eclipse* and a work in the now defunct MuroSur gallery. This exhibition, then, is intended as a representative overview of the artist's output, and the choice of works is designed to acquaint the Chilean public with its different phases, formats, and subjects. It can be regarded as a kind of anthology, a way of introducing and presenting an output that is far vaster than what can be shown here, even in an exhibition as generous as the one now offered in the exhibition spaces of Telefónica Chile and Galería Gabriela Mistral. The aim is to bring Chilean viewers into contact with some of the visual statements made by the artist over the years: works that are particularly well known because of their international impact, such as *A Logo for America* and *Lament of the Images*, but also those that are closest to us in time, such as the *Gramsci Trilogy* and *Muxima*, works that Chilean viewers will discover for the first time.

In the "Conversations" included in this volume, the artist explains how the works that were to come to Chile were selected, considering that they would be shown in indoor venues and thus that, with one exception—*A Logo for America*—his public interventions could not be included. He wanted to show his most recent works, but also those that had had the greatest impact in Chile and yet were known only by hearsay to most viewers in this country. He also wanted work that would be representative of the fundamental issues he had been reflecting on throughout his career. What we shall find in this exhibition, then, is an overview of his work, including the pieces which have had the greatest international repercussions—*A Logo for America* and *Lament of the Images*; the most recent, namely *The Gramsci Trilogy* and *Muxima*, which so far this year has been presented in New York, at the Hirschorn Museum in Washington, at the Biarritz festival, at the Fundación Tàpies, and at the Reina Sofía Museum in Madrid; and pieces representative of his work in Africa, *The Silence of Nduwayezu*; Asia, *Untitled (water)*; and Latin America, *Out of Balance*. Traversing all of these, we can recognize different approaches to subjects of vital importance to the artist, such as his thinking about images, his questioning of the role of artists and intellectuals in contemporary societies, and his determination to create an "aesthetics of resistance." [2] This selection also provides a representative sample of the different formats he has employed, with tremendous capacity for renewal and change, over the last twenty years.

This book

This book, which marks an encounter between Alfredo Jaar's work and Chile, opens with something completely new. *Chile, 1981, Before Leaving* is an intervention recorded here in images for the very first time. It consisted of a line of small Chilean flags planted across the whole width of the country, from mountains to sea; a line of flags that divided the country, or perhaps made its division visually apparent. The flags traversing the dunes and then running across an immense beach and down into the water are a shuddering reminder of the bodies thrown into the sea, of those who were exiled and incarcerated in the Pisagua landscape, of so many other images that were emerging then and that were to leave an indelible imprint on the nation's memory. And they are a moving testimony to the spirit of someone who is departing, the record in earth and water, mountain and sea, of a small, fluttering farewell. A secret the artist kept until now, until a reunion could come about.

The texts had to be written in Chile. That meant making a choice: putting aside the bibliography published in major world centers, and even the earlier books written about the artist's works. It was, I repeat, a reunion. With me, Adriana Valdés, the author of the first text on his work (1981) and an "essential friendship" ever since, according to Alfredo Jaar;[3] but mainly with the new thinking in our country, with what is happening right now when the younger generations talk about art. In a way, I could read into this choice a determination that reminded me of another book organized by the artist, *Emergencia*, based on his work of the same title about Africa. The idea then was not to talk about the continent, but to give a platform to its own writers, to "give them back… conversation and dialogue." There is something of that in this book. It contains the results of the conversation and dialogue that took place between Alfredo Jaar, his work and ideas, and the team that prepared the book, all participants in the postgraduate program at the Faculty of Arts of the University of Chile. A critical emergence, and an emergency too. Elsewhere in the world, writing had been produced to deal with this challenging body of work. It was urgent to do it also in Chile, from Chile. And it was good that the new writing should come from those who are beginning to distinguish themselves as young thinkers about art in our country.

A.V.

[1] Alfredo Jaar, *The Fire This Time: Public Interventions 1979-2005*, Milan, Charta, 2005.
[2] This is the title of his recent publication on the *Gramsci Trilogy*, Como, Fondazione Antonio Ratti and ACTAR, 2005.
[3] In *Studies on Happiness 1979-1981*, Barcelona, ACTAR, 1999.

JAAR
SCL
2006

One warm spring morning in 1996, their Royal Highnesses the King and Queen of Spain, Don Juan Carlos and Doña Sofía, inaugurated the modern Compañía de Telecomunicaciones de Chile corporate building, by Plaza Italia, in the heart of Santiago.

The ground floor of the building, then known as the CTC Tower, was designed with a feeling of fondness toward the city and its inhabitants: a space open to the community, housing a splendid auditorium along with a large, generous space for mounting art exhibitions. Time has flown since then: in these ten years the Sala de Arte Fundación Telefónica has become a central part of national artistic expression. It has held more than fifty exhibitions, and has had more than two million local and foreign visitors.

To celebrate these ten years, Fundación Telefónica Chile is pleased to present the first individual exhibition by Alfredo Jaar in Chile in twenty-five years: JAAR SCL 2006.

We are proud to offer the community an exhibition which, because of the artist's trajectory as well as the relevance, importance and solidity of the works on show, so many Chileans have been looking forward to.

For years Chile has been indebted to Alfredo Jaar. That he should bring to his native land nine of his works, that he—along with international figures—should indulge us with his Semana Crítica (Critical Week) of sessions aimed at reflecting on and seeking answers to the timeless questions regarding the meaning of art before a diverse public, is an honour for which we are thankful.

This is, without doubt, a privilege and it is our way of paying tribute to our achievements over these ten years—and to the artist's over more than twenty-five, most of them realized beyond our borders and (why not admit it?) for many years outside the national art scene and thus beyond its recognition. Precisely in this regard, we hope that the publication of this volume will prove to be a contribution to the historiography of Chilean visual arts.

What moves the spectator is not just the reality which makes itself unavoidable in each piece by Alfredo Jaar, but also the beauty and clarity with which the artist articulates his discourse, resorting to the word and to silence; the image and its absence; light and darkness; rhythm, juxtaposition and spatial order in the installations, and cinematic order in his most recent work, *Muxima*.

The invitation remains open—for whomever wants truly to look—to question oneself, to explore the themes posed in the show and, ultimately, to involve oneself in social issues, coming into profound contact with the horrors of which human history is wrought: the abuse of power, the scandalous inequality between rich and poor, the pain and—of course—the hope as well.

The mission of a company like Fundación Telefónica Chile is precisely to connect all Chileans, throughout our land, as well as serving as a bridge between its inhabitants and the rest of the world. Nonetheless, we like to take a more ambitious view of our job: we join the country together, facilitating its development and growth. Which is why we have provided decisive support for the diffusion of art and culture, essential vehicles of communication.

Francisco Aylwin Oyarzún
Executive Director
Fundación Telefónica – Chile

I dedicate this return to Chile to my father
Alfredo Jaar (1920-2002) and my mother Miriam.
Infinite gratitude for giving me (the) light.

Works 1980-2006

1980 >

Studies on Happiness 01

Studies on Happiness 04

1981 >

Studies on Happiness 07

Chile, 1981, before leaving

1983 >

The Silence

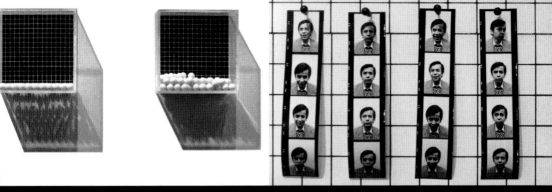

Studies on Happiness 02

Studies on Happiness 03

Studies on Happiness 05

Studies on Happiness 06

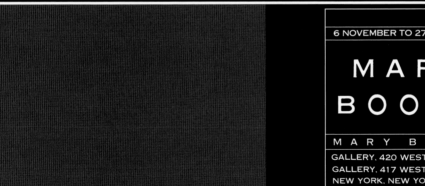

1982 >

Mary Boone

Monument for South America

Colors

1984 >

Businessweek Magazine Cover, Dec 24, 1984

Freedom in America. What Freedom, What America?

The Power of Words 02

1986 >

Welcome to the Third World 01

Gold in the Morning 02

Rushes

You and Us

The Power of Words 01

1985 >

Gold in the Morning 01

Welcome to the Third World 02

Welcome to the Third World 03

Persona

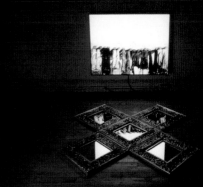

The Silence

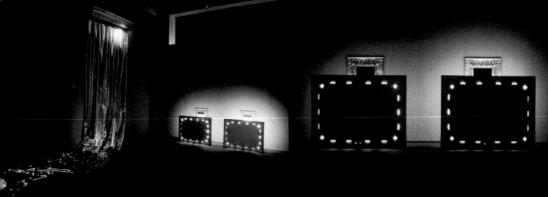

Frame of Mind 03

Frame of Mind 04

1988 >

Михаил Горбаче

A Star is Born

Gesamtkunstwerk

Coyote 01

Frame of Mind 01

Frame of Mind 02

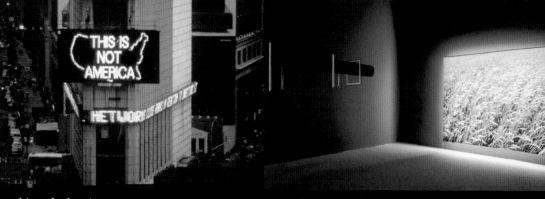

A Logo for America

Learning to Play

Contents

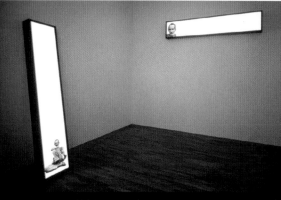

Cries and Whispers

Coyote 02

Coyote 03

Coyote 04

Modernism is Dead, Long Live Modernism

Welcome to Canada

Fading

Falling Rocks 01

Falling Rocks 02

Out of Balance

Paysage

1989 >

The Booth

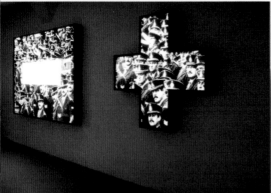

No More

Reflections

Hope, Happiness and Freedom

La Géographie ça sert d'abord à faire la Guerre

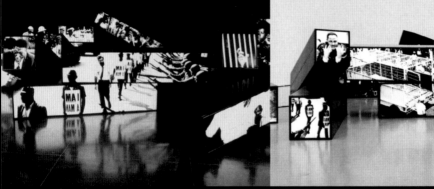

The Fire Next Time

They loved it so much, the Revolution 01

They loved it so much, the Revolution 02

1990 >

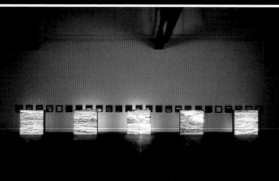

Untitled (Water)

Memories of Underdevelopment

Opening New Doors

Fading

HÉ RAM

Terra Non Descoperta 01

The Body is the Map

El Dia Que Me Quieras

Spheres of Influence

1991 >

Geography = War 01

Geography = War 02

Terra Non Descoperta 04

Lagos 2002

The Way It Was

1992 >

The Aesthetics of Resistance 02

The Conference

Two or three Things I imagine about Them 01

Two or three Things I imagine about Them 02

Museum

Saturday Night

1968

The Aesthetics of Resistance 01

Je Me Souviens

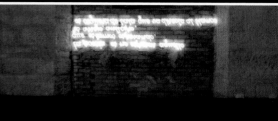

Rafael, Manuel y los otros

Two or three Things I imagine about Them 03

Unframed 01

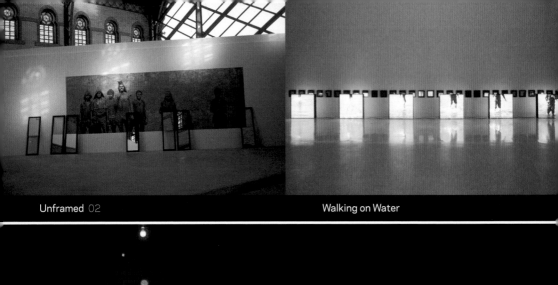

Unframed 02   Walking on Water

Blow-Up   Bonjour Sécurité

Repetition   1994 >

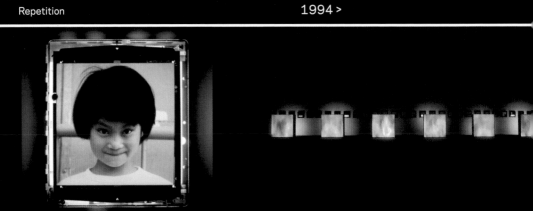

A Hundred Times Nguyen 03   Europa

1993 >

Working

Crossing

Fading

A Hundred Times Nguyen 01

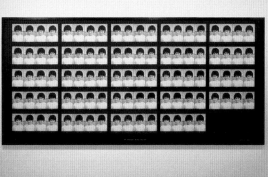

A Hundred Times Nguyen 02

Signs of Life

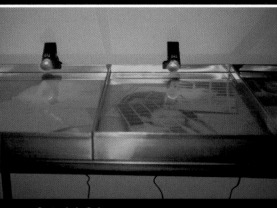

Serie de la Sal

Rwanda, Rwanda

1995 >

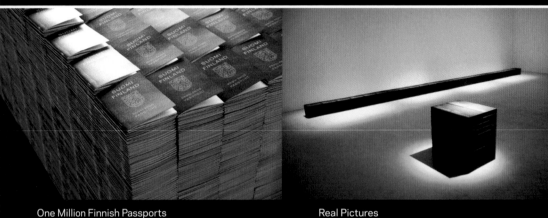

One Million Finnish Passports

Real Pictures

1996 >

Camera Lucida

Shelter (Please Close Your Eyes)

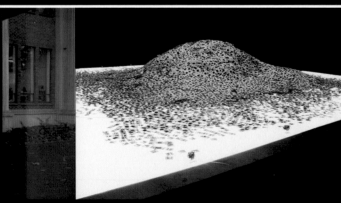

The Eyes of Gutete Emerita 01

100.000 DEATHS

Slide and Sound

Teach us to Outgrow our Madness

Homage

Let there be Light

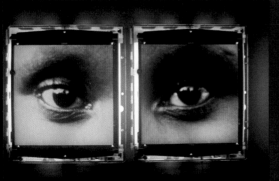

Over a five month period in 1994, more than one million Rwandans, mostly members of the Tutsi minority, were systematically slaughtered as the world closed its eyes to genocide. The killings were largely carried out by Hutu militias who had been armed and trained by the Rwandan

The Eyes of Gutete Emerita 02

The Eyes of Gutete Emerita 03

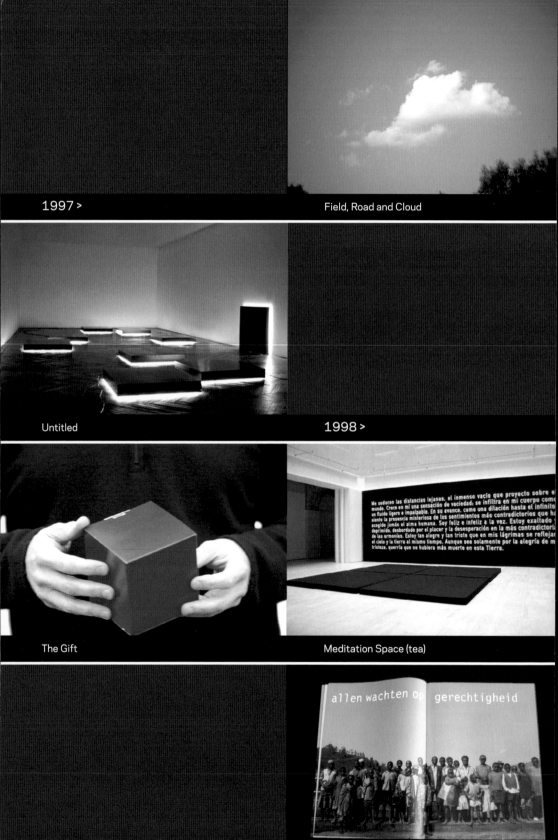

1997 >

Field, Road and Cloud

Untitled

1998 >

The Gift

Meditation Space (tea)

Me seducen las distancias lejanas, el inmenso vacío que proyecto sobre el
mundo. Crece en mí una sensación de vaciedad; se infiltra en mi cuerpo como
un fluido ligero e impalpable. En su avance, como una dilación hasta el infinito
siento la presencia misteriosa de los sentimientos más contradictorios que ha
acogido jamás el alma humana. Soy feliz e infeliz a la vez. Estoy exaltado y
deprimido, desbordado por el placer y la desesperación en la más contradictoria
de las armonías. Estoy tan alegre y tan triste que en mis lágrimas se reflejan
el cielo y la tierra al mismo tiempo. Aunque sea solamente por la alegría de mi
tristeza, querría que no hubiera más muerte en esta Tierra.

allen wachten op gerechtigheid

It is Difficult

The Silence of Nduwayezu

Emergencia

Epilogue

Meditation Space (coffee)

Weltanschauung

Lights in the City

Playground

Waiting
2000 >

Offering

Signs of Light

2001 >

The Silence

Walking 01

Lament of the Images 01

Bunka no Hako (Culture Box)

The Cloud

Six Seconds

The Skoghall Konsthall

The Spectacle of Life

2002 >

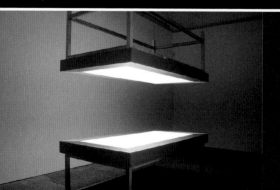

Walking 02

Project Emergencia

Project for a Revolution

Searching for Gramsci

Let One Hundred Flowers Bloom

The Ashes of Gramsci

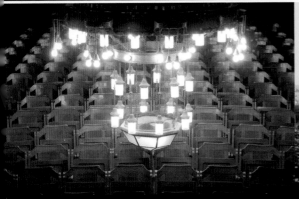

Requiem for Leipzig

Muxima

Hope

2004 >

Infinite Cell

2005 >

The Aesthetics of Resistance

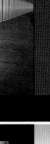

La Geografia del Futuro

2006 >

The Sound of Silence

"Don't think like an artist, think like a human being"

Notes for a poetics of Alfredo Jaar

Adriana Valdés

Alfredo Jaar's work has its own poetics, its own aesthetic: it comes from the passion that drives him and not from the precepts of the day. He is a great reader, a restless reader, and he has many interests, but art criticism and theory are not prominent among them: as a specialization, they leave him cold. He is not a follower of market fashions – or of fashions in theory – and his work is not easy to place in the classifications of the manuals. Ask him about this, and his reply is as telling as it is succinct: "I don't care."

If we are to seek for his poetics,[1] then, we must do so in the power of his practice. It is in his works that we shall be able to discern its true lineaments. Sometimes a clear referentiality may appear—in the *Studies on Happiness* (1979-1981, in Chile), for instance, which invite comparisons with Haacke and Fluxus—but the tendency, the transformations, derive from impulses which are not those of the world of art. We might even venture to say that one of his great early metaphors, in works such as *1+1+1*, shown at Documenta in 1987, or *Unframed*, among many others, comes from the need to break out of the framework of art. As though it were the limitations and conventions framing the space of art that had to be shown for what they were, and transcended.

One way to break out of this framework is to be constantly exploring new media and formats. The key to what drives him is to be found not in an insistence on any particular one, but precisely in his need to transcend them. This need is linked to an imperative that comes from the "outside" of art. "I don't know if it's because of my training, but I've never been able to create a single work of art that isn't a response to something real. I can't do it. I'm a project artist, not a studio artist."[2] Jaar's architectural training is a decisive influence on the language he uses to describe what he does. He treats the "something real" as a "problem"—and each work is the outcome of a series of planned activities, including first-hand research and all the stages of production and assembly. How the work is actually made depends on all sorts of factors to which formalism is completely irrelevant; depends, essentially, on the nature of the problem, the reality he is addressing in each case. This explains the startling creativity we find as we review his work over the years. Each "problem" leads him to explore a different format, using different media, including the most technologically advanced. In this case, the artistic project does not lag behind media developments; sometimes it actually has to wait for the technology that will make it possible. "I'm a believer in the power of ideas [...] No technical or domestic or administrative problem will stand in my way [...] I have a project that waited ten years to become technically feasible: it opens in March," he says in the "Conversations" included in the present volume.[3]

The diversity of the media used, though, is not the deepest layer in this metaphor of frames, this "unframing" of art. In Jaar's work there is a palpable need to consider art and life together. "Life is more important than art," to use a quote Jaar himself employs, "that's what makes art important."[4] This approach does not sit easily with a number of the attitudes that seem to inform art today. This is not self-absorbed art[5] in dialogue with itself, "art for art's sake," or an art whose subject-matter, after more than half a century, is still its own bankruptcy,[6] its own emptiness—or, more recently, here in Chile, its own capitulation to the market and to decoration. Nor is it inspired by the old avant-garde dream of producing "emancipatory" effects by desublimating a meaning or destructuring a form[7] or, most emphatically, by that melancholy detachment, ultimately despairing, in which art mourns for itself—or at least for its possible function in the life of society, now reduced to "bearing interminable witness to the immemorial alienation that makes every promise of emancipation a lie..."[8] Underlying the impeccable surfaces of Jaar's work, its meticulous effects, and its highly rational organization, are a greater urgency and a greater vitality. Where this work comes from, art is not a self-sufficient calling.

Unframing, visibilizing, visualizing

Where the world of art is concerned, then, "unframing" means bringing into that world what lies outside it. In Santiago, Chile, in 1979-1981, at the height of the dictatorship, this meant bringing in the street, the public space permeated at that time by fear; making viewers' faces appear on screen (a novelty at the time) and leading them on to talk, drawing them out of their traditional contemplative muteness (and, in that political climate, making them vote). In New York, it meant taking faces from the "outside," those of the Serra Pelada miners photographed by Jaar himself in Brazil, and placing them in the subway stations of Wall Street (a world center for the trade in the gold extracted by these miners) and on the immaculate walls of galleries and museums. This gesture of bringing in the faces and figures of the "outside" is repeated in many of his works from the period, and those who appear are from different parts of the world, from the different crucibles of suffering and conflict that are largely what make any kind of aloof skepticism possible—including that of the New York art world.

We may speak, then, of a *drive for visibilization*. This does not just mean *visualization*, the artistic organization of the materials for a work, although it includes that too. It means *visibilizing*, conferring visibility upon something that does not form part of viewers' habitual way of thinking, something that disturbs them and throws them off balance, something that seems foreign to them... yet at the same time draws them in somehow, drives a wedge of unease into their systems of certainties. *A Hundred Times Nguyen*, for example, visibilizes the fate of Vietnamese refugees in Hong Kong.[9] The potential for making this situation politically visible depends on how it is visualized, what resources are used to make it exist, effectively and affectively, for the viewer. The resource used is poetic: in a book without words, other than a half-page of information at the end, four photographs—beautiful, perfect, and almost identical—of a small Vietnamese girl looking rather impishly into the camera are repeated to a total of one hundred. There is nothing dramatic about the photos, far from it. Only the reiteration adds the *pathos* which turns this innocent image into an obsessive memory, an open question about the future, a painful concern, finally a responsibility that is hard to pin down and is harrowing for this very reason.

There is a reference worth dusting off here. Critics of literature, of poetry, used to speak of the "objective correlative" of an emotion: "a set of objects, a situation, a chain of events which shall be the formula of that *particular* emotion; such that when the external facts, which must terminate in sensory experience, are given, the emotion is immediately evoked."[10] Nothing could be further from their author's intention, but these words could perfectly well describe the process of visualization in a work by Alfredo Jaar. The intention is to *visibilize* a situation that induces an emotional response. The *visualization* process, meanwhile, consists in finding that "objective correlative" which, in the work (an installation, for example), succeeds in conveying a knowledge of that situation while at the same time inducing in the viewer a response which transcends this knowledge: a response which is, moreover, emotional. The word "emotion" comes from the Latin *emovere*, which relates to movement. In this case, that meaning should be preferred over that of a merely sentimental response. "Bodily movements and mental reactions—every way in which they physically engage the viewer, really—should ultimately lead to another type of engagement," says the artist about his installations.[11] And he adds: "The works that best achieve their objective [...] give us an aesthetic experience, they give us information, and they ask us to react. And the depth of the reaction will depend on the ability of the work to move us both through our senses and through our reason, a very difficult combination, and one that is almost impossible to pull off."[12]

It is only through recognition that we are constituted as socially viable beings.[13] To visibilize is to confer recognition. The passion for visibilization runs right through Jaar's work and is visualized—is staged, visually resolved—in the most varying ways, depending on what "problems" are being addressed in each case.

The public intervention *Lights in the City* (Montreal, 1999) visibilizes homeless men each time they enter a shelter by triggering a red light that illuminates from within a huge dome visible from many parts of the city. It compels recognition of their existence and the makeshift circumstances they live in, while respectfully preserving their anonymity. The names of places in Rwanda that were projected in lights on to public buildings in France (*Signs of Light*, Lyons, 2000) is another example: the staging is different, but there is an analogous urge to compel recognition of something that has been relegated to the blind spots of our collective experience. And the many works in the Rwanda project mark a very important turning point in Jaar's approach to the problems of visualization, as will be seen later. For now, it is the desire to provoke recognition that I would like to stress, as this holds a very sensitive place in Jaar's poetics, a place where poetics and politics (to use the latter term in its widest and most generous sense) enter into a relationship that I would like to call *radiant*. [14]

Politics, poetics, ethics

For politics, as someone once said, is imagination or it is nothing; [15] it has to be imagination, or else it is just a predictable and rather shabby round of trade-offs between well-established interests. Jaar's work situates his passion for visibilizing, for creating recognition, at the very point where imagination is grafted into politics. It is not a comfortable place, as he is the first to acknowledge. "And works fail [...] How do you strike such a perfect balance that it's informative, moving, inspires people to think and act... I've no idea how you do it. But that's what we're working on. If there's anything more political than that..." [16]

Recognition is a profoundly political subject. The fact is that the conditions by which we are recognized as human are socially constructed, and sometimes the very terms that confer "humanness" on some individuals are those that deprive certain other individuals of it, producing a difference between the human and the less than human. Then, recognition "becomes a site of power by which the human is differentially produced." [17] If there's anything more political than that... Examples abound. Political opponents were not human in the Chile of the dictatorship; therefore they were not recognized as having human rights. [18] Immigrants – in Europe, the United States, Hong Kong – are less human than the rest. And Africa – this is what emerges from the twenty plus works included in Jaar's Rwanda project – is a whole continent whose inhabitants are not entirely human: for one hundred days, the massacre of a million people was invisible to the so-called international community.

Being invisible. Being there but unseen. Being transparent, so that people look straight through you without seeing you. Being the blind spot in the other's field of vision... In different formats, Jaar's work as an artist returns to this situation again and again. [19] To visibilize, then, is unquestionably a political task: the task of identifying some of the huge zones of denial on which our image of the public realm is based. But it is not only a political task. In these works, it is inseparable from the poetic imagination, in the widest sense: a form of thinking with materials. [20] The staging, the visualization, brings into play a way of thinking that is not verbal but visual. This appeals to that part of us which cannot be encompassed by our understanding alone; that drive in us which we do not and cannot know; a dimension of ourselves, and of our relationship with others, in which our urges are neither exclusively biological nor exclusively cultural, "but always the site of their dense convergence." [21]

To move viewers is to affect them all the way to that suprarational dimension—to wrench them out of their passive observer's attitude, make them feel, in a way, observed, appealed to by the work. At best, it is to make them burst out, like Rilke at the end of his famous sonnet to a torso of Apollo: "You must change your life." In that sonnet, it is the torso of Apollo that watches the poet. Not the statue's eyes: it is just a torso, it has lost its head and limbs. In the beauty of that body, though, "there is no place that does not see you," says the poem. [22]

Beauty is a complex subject and one that tends to be repressed in current thinking about art. Some critics, seen as more conservative, eloquently defend it as pleasure, opposing it to a contemporary "sublime" dedicated to mortification and hostile to the embellishment of harsh truths. [23] Others analyze it as ornamentation and falsification. In many debates, the subject is simply ignored. The impact of Jaar's work allows it to be approached in a different way. Here, beauty has a primordial function, connected above all with the power of the works' appeal. [24] More than just ornamentation or pleasure, the laconic and usually minimalist beauty of Jaar's works is what he calls its "poetic" dimension, and is in fact one more dimension of thought—the one, that is, which "the work expresses in non-verbal ways," [25] the specific difference that sets it apart from information.

This "poetic" quality can be found in the most subtle aspects of Jaar's artistic operations. Essays in the present book speak of the "material vocation" of his works, the "mesh of light" as a "perennial infrastructure" underlying them, their "unashamedly physical" character, their "somatic, aesthetic quality [...] this almost non-material, infraphysical level of the reflection, the wake, the dispersed light." [26] There are references as well to a "liquid drift of the eye" that is also "an invitation to reconsider the set parameters wherein the very act of looking is organized."[27] It is in these dimensions and others like them that Jaar combines a reflectiveness and an awareness that easily transcend the restrained language of information, necessary and present in his work though this is. "You can't get the news from poems / yet men die miserably every day / for lack of what is found there;" Jaar has staged these lines by William Carlos Williams both in the introduction to his impressive web site and in an earlier public work.[28] In them, "news" may be equivalent to information; but what poems give us is not to be found there, and without what poems have to give, the existence of mortals is miserable.

To think of Jaar's work as an exercise in protest and nothing more is to miss a dimension that is absolutely indispensable—and is the most interesting, the most mysterious, the most radiant. It is the one that affects people not just in their political aspect, not just in their artistic aspect, but in their humanity, which is more than the sum of the two. "Don't think like an artist, think like a human being," says Jaar, as though in passing.[29] The "poetic" quality creates works in which human beings are seen—like Rilke before the torso of Apollo—"from the body of the god," from the compulsion of every faculty, from their capacity for wonder, from their "highest vocation," which, as Danto says of a work by Barbara Kruger, is "something more than sitting on its ass in some museum or other."[30] It is a very demanding perspective. From it we understand better the quote of Godard's that tends to come up in Alfredo Jaar's interviews: "It may be true that one has to choose between ethics and aesthetics, but it is no less true that whichever one chooses, one will always find the other at the end of the road."

"A critical poet of the politics of the image"
This artist's work has always given us much to think about in relation to the staging of images. As he said in an interview, for him any aesthetic decision is also an ethical decision, and the way images are presented, their beauty, the way they appear, their relationship with light, are more than visual solutions: they are also a form of thought in which the visual aspect is critical. Approaching works presented almost twenty years ago—I am thinking of *La géographie, ça sert d'abord à faire la guerre* (1987)—I was able to speak at the time of an "aesthetic of the elusive image." At issue was the fixity of photographic images and their relationship with the way things were perceived from a position of power, of domination. Reflections (in mirrors, in water), the variability of the images depending on exactly where the viewer stood, the elements shown fleetingly and scarcely glimpsed, I saw as being intended to preserve the ambiguity of the image. As for the mobility with which

Jaar's work traversed borders and cultures, I read this as a constantly renewed effort to avoid a fixity of perception, to save himself from the petrification that overtakes the unmoving regard of an observer who perceives himself as a wielder of power from the center. And as a reflective way of respecting the radical differences between human beings... An ethics of the other, of otherness, could be inferred from this type of visual reflection. [31]

Years later, this reflective concern was still there, was intensifying, indeed, and about to take a radical turn. In 1994, the year of his first journey to Rwanda, the *Europa* exhibition was held in Stuttgart. In the book that accompanied it, the Catalan poet Vicenç Altaió wrote: "Images have an advanced religion: they bury history." It is a phrase that resonates in Jaar's work: as if he had been reading it ever since—and staging its multiple readings.

With the Rwanda project, a dramatic awareness that had already been hinted at in Jaar's work was crystallized: an awareness of the inability of images to convey horror. The thousands of photographs Jaar took after the genocide were not shown. *Real Pictures* was a work that visualized the impossibility of showing them: the installation had a funeral quality, the exhibits were like above-ground sepulchers. Inside each one was a photograph whose presence was signaled by a short but descriptive text. Holding back the pictures was a way of removing them from circulation. To publicize the images of horror would have been to trivialize them, cast them into the media vortex where such things perish: as spectators, we watch them go by with the indifference of those who feel no responsibility for anything, of whom nothing is expected but to watch and wait for the next stimulus, while their threshold of insensitivity, their ability to inure themselves against any appeal, steadily rises. The disjunction between seeing and participating, between seeing and engaging, is the characteristic of a society turned spectacle. Vaclav Havel, the writer and first president of the Czech Republic, said that a person who felt no responsibility for anything other than his personal survival "is a demoralized person. The system depends on this demoralization, deepens it, it is in fact a projection of it into society." [32]

The visualization of each work, its format, its aesthetic, is inextricably linked, then, to the ethical stance it takes—it is tempting to say that Jaar's poetics is to be found precisely in that site of "dense convergence" between the two. This site is different in each work. Each staging assays a different approach to the unmentionable.

"It was one attempt more," says Jaar, referring to *The Silence of Nduwayezu*. "Then I despaired again," he adds, "and went off to look for another format." [33] The twenty plus works in the Rwanda project speak of this despair, the *pathos* of images which, for all their potency, are bound to fail. "To wage battle as though it mattered" is a noble old precept, and it is echoed by a phrase of Gramsci's which Alfredo Jaar often quotes: "pessimism of the intelligence, optimism of the will." The search for new formats, new media, new visualizations needs to be understood in the light of Jaar's pessimism, but of his optimism also, the twin poles of an urgent need that is ethical and aesthetic at once.

Lament of the Images, the installation that became famous at Documenta 11, in 2002, is a work in which the "critical poet of the politics of the image" shines radiantly through.[34] Jaar's long-standing reflection on the image in today's world is given dramatic and complex expression here. The installation mingles the themes of captivity, that of people and that of images; the dazzling effect of an excess of light; power, both economic and political; real and symbolic violence. The work brings almost every element of this reflection into play, in an economical and highly effective synthesis. And it stages the paradox of excessive visibility which, by accumulation, means that we ultimately see nothing, or only what the very powerful allow us to see. *Lament...* is an elegy to the possibility of criticizing the politics of the image, and at the same time a powerful admonition, a visibilization of what the media glitter surrounding us conceals, a harrowing experience of the limits to what can be achieved.

It is also something more than that. The distress caused by the status of images in today's society of spectacle—or control[35]—is compounded by the ethical distress arising from the observer's or artist's own status. The fact is that, in these societies, the observer or artist is in the predicament of being "part victim, part accomplice, like everyone else."[36] There is no "place apart" from which the artist can speak as a prophet, no position of moral superiority peculiar to him. Nor is there a totalizing narrative to provide him with justification. Talking about *Untitled (water)*, the artist accepts this. "I put these images in your world, but always in a fragmented form, so that my inability to show everything becomes part of the work. As does the dilemma it meant for me to spend several days on the ships that were being used by the immigration authority [...] I accept my privileged position of having taken the photos, and then I leave."[37] This dramatic involvement of the artist in the very situation he deplores does not occur only on the plane of action. It is also there in the constant need to re-examine the conditions of looking and seeing, and to continue exploring and probing the contradictions by staging his paradoxical challenge to the very images which are his material.[38]

Artist, intellectual, human being

Jaar persists—pessimism of the intelligence, but optimism of the will—in seeking to make art function in the life of society, and not just in specialist circles. The purpose is to avoid a situation characteristic of contemporary art which is amusingly depicted by Ana María Risco in the "Conversations": being "like people riding an exercise bike: puffing away, but getting nowhere." The desire to reach an "outside" of art where art can acquire a function larger than itself shapes the very organization of Jaar's activities. He gives only a third of his time to his work in galleries and museums; another third is devoted to public art, and the last third to teaching. This is so that he will not end up by treating art as just "a game for initiates which... leaves out anyone still capable of being affected by it!" [39]

Public art takes the artist away from the protected, controlled environment of galleries and museums and exposes him to reactions and to the unexpected. "Jaar's art seems at its most ambitious and complex when it begins to lose control, produce unanticipated effects and raise doubts in the mind of the viewer," [40] says a critic about the remarkable project *The Skoghall Konsthall*, in Sweden. The same might have been said earlier of *Camera lucida*, a project conducted in a Caracas neighborhood, or his most recent project in the city of Leipzig. What all three works do is visibilize a need that is not explicitly recognized by a human group. The splendid wood and paper museum is solemnly inaugurated with the authorities in attendance and an exhibition of young artists, but it is made only to be burned down the next day: what the flames are meant to illuminate is the total absence in Skoghall of any facilities for meeting and thinking, for artistic and creative communication; it is up to its inhabitants to create them. In Catia, Caracas, the task was to open the museum which had been built instead of the soccer pitch the neighborhood wanted—and this was done by distributing disposable cameras and film and holding an exhibition in which the local people were both the photographers and the photographed, taking full possession of a place from which they might have felt excluded, themselves appropriating the museum. With the Leipzig project, staged in an abandoned church in a neighborhood likewise excluded from the promise of prosperity held out by German unification, spectators watch from their benches as a huge, gleaming antique lamp descends very slowly to eye level, to the strains of a cantata by Bach, a Leipzig musician... "I thought this was going to stir up discussion," confided the artist, "but the discussion always happened outside." [41] In these three projects, separated as they were in time and space, and despite their use of totally different "solutions" where images were concerned, there lies a meaning that is inseparable from Jaar's work, one of the drives that dominate and shape it.

This is the appeal —utopian though it may be—for a "being-in-common," [42] for a civic practice, a solidarity, that is capable of creating engagement; a practice different in each place and time, specific and local, like each of these works. An appeal to "use what we have to invent what we desire." [43]

In all these cases, the artist uses what he has—the prerogatives of art—to invent what he desires. He sees the world of art as a beleaguered preserve of freedom where, for now, it is still possible to think in utopian terms. "I find it so natural to do it there. I wouldn't know what else to do," he says. And adds: "It's true that in the world of art you really can think very subversively. Now, whether that actually affects reality is a different matter. At least we can offer models, take a utopian view." [44]

The role and fate of the intellectual in today's society is what this view encompasses in the five works forming the *Gramsci Trilogy*, [45] one of his most recent works, made to be shown in present-day Italy where, according to the artist, fascism is in the air. Three historical figures are drawn into a symbolic game from which none emerges unaltered. *Let One Hundred Flowers Bloom* is a phrase used by Mao in a temporary relaxation of his tyranny, when he invited intellectuals to declare themselves, create, produce ideas, come out into the light. The outcome is well known: more tyranny, persecutions and disasters. Ideas survive like the flowers in the installation, tortured by hostile conditions, by cold, inclement winds. *Infinite Cell* is a symbolic allusion, first and foremost, to Gramsci's years of imprisonment under fascism. And the third figure is the important film-maker Pier Paolo Pasolini, from whose poem *Le ceneri di Gramsci* ("The Ashes of Gramsci") the title of another work is taken, [46] and whose murder has never been solved. From the intermingling of these figures, we come to see the role and fate of the intellectual in terms of great suffering, conflict and uncertainty.

Gramsci was, among many other things, an acute analyst of the relationship between intellectuals, artists and politics. But these works of Jaar's are not exactly a reverential tribute, an effort to recover and reformulate ideas such as we m-ight expect in an academic seminar. They have a relationship of urgency, of emergency, with the present. As though the past could only be contemplated from the standpoint of an oppressive present (one of this artist's early works contained a short text: "If not him, who? And if not now, when?"). There is no attempt to recreate the historical conditions of Gramsci's thought, just as it is not claimed that the *Infinite Cell* is a replica of the cell Gramsci was imprisoned in. Rather, the cell is taken as an idea, a symbol, that is far more than just a reference to past history. The cell becomes the metaphor for the condition of art and thought in a society of which Gramsci could form only a tentative, remote idea.

The effort to give thought an "organic" role in a society's progress was utopian even then: now, in the society of media images, it is so to a degree that can only be described as tragic. [47] *Infinite Cell* could, like earlier works of Jaar's, have been called *Meditation Space*. Its infiniteness suggests the inexorable incarceration of intellectual and artistic activity today, its suicidal self-referentiality, its compartmentalization and specialization (many years ago, Edward Said remarked that the specialization of academic critical thinking was a kind of incarceration in which each discipline was a ghetto, and that there was a huge gap between each of them, which was being filled at that time "by television and Reagan"). It also suggests, paradoxically, the infiniteness of thought, the infinite capacity of the human mind. And the numerous moments in history that have seen "the profound naïve struggle to make / life over collapse in ruins," in the words of Pier Paolo Pasolini.

Searching for Gramsci is a photographic pilgrimage that ends at the thinker's tomb, which is also the setting for the poem written by Pasolini in 1954. It is a moving piece, whose allusion to "the silence, humid, fruitless" charges the reference to the "hundred flowers" of Mao's appeal, which speaks of "loving the world I hate" and asks "but what's the use of such light," meaning the light of history. The *Trilogy*, conceived as a series of opportunities for meditation on the role of art and artists, is both a despairing reflection and an appeal. In this text I would like to see it, too, as an opportunity for meditation on Jaar's poetics, on his work as an artist, on his profound ethical imperative and, at the same time, on his lucid and unyielding diagnosis of art and intellectuals at the present time.

Lastly, *Muxima*, his most recent work, forges a new path in terms of the medium used. [48] It is the first time Alfredo Jaar has made a film. Its subject matter, once again, is Africa. It deals specifically with the situation of Angola, a former Portuguese colony that still bears the marks of its colonial past and of a present that can only be called neo-colonialist. AIDS, the brutal exploitation of natural resources which enrich only a handful, buried anti-personnel mines, environmental pollution, all this is shown and condemned by the work. But this film, lasting a little over thirty minutes, is something far more complex than a condemnation.

Unlike a normal documentary, the film has no voiceover. There is no unifying narrative or identifiable linear continuity. Continuity is provided, above all, by the music: in breath made rhythm, in the rhythms constituting communal memory crystallized in voice and song, the "dense convergence," once more, of words, memory, shared emotion. The relationship with poetry is made explicit by its structure—it is divided into "Cantos," short, unconnected visual episodes. And, most importantly, it employs the resources of the cinema in a way that, to this visual artist, proves mind-blowing. First, the sound track is structured from multiple versions, produced at different times, of just one song from the country, *Muxima* (the word means "heart"), punctuated by the near-silence of the events on the screen. Second, editing and montage are used to create new kinds of connections between images. And the viewers' attention is held by it for more than half an hour, in total isolation from everything else around them. The average amount of time spent looking at a work in an exhibition is statistically derisory and, for a visual artist, creating a film means foraying into a wholly different medium of expression and exploring new possibilities of presentation, new ways of moving the viewer.

And finally

Perhaps without quite meaning to, I have come back to the key word in this essay. "Move." To set in motion, unite in a movement, produce a deep impression that is not confined to personal feelings alone but spills over into a common emotion. "Emotion is what brings us into contact with the pre-individual."[49] To appeal to a sense of community, seemingly impossible though it may be: to a "being-in-common" as remote as the God of the negative theologies, resplendent only by his absence. To a sense of community so utopian that only the resources of art can now call it up... Of art as *poiesis*, art as doing, as a summoning forth, an invocation even—using this word in its magical, radiant sense.

Alfredo Jaar's poetics has very important implications for the current art scene. To see what these are, it may be necessary to proceed by way of contrast. His stubborn faith in "reiterating poetry,"[50] in waging battle by means of work whose format, in his eyes, is always inadequate but always open to the next, could not be further from the sophisticated and rather cynical resignation of an art that is happy to regard itself as impotent and dying, and that has now been broadcasting the news of its own demise for so many years. Again, to describe this drive as "romantic" merely highlights another fundamental contrast: Jaar's work will have nothing to do with the exaltation of the ego so characteristic of the committed romantics who, in Shelley's words, "sing to cheer their own solitude with sweet sounds." What shines out from this poetics are not the burning eyes of the poet, "sickly now from burning so long," a poet half-inclined to see himself as a prophetic bearer of truth. From the standpoint of Jaar's poetics, such a character would certainly have a touch of fascism about him. In the Leipzig work, the light illuminates no one but the viewers themselves. The light has been descending slowly to eye level, and that is the point where all eyes meet. These eyes are not lifted heavenward in religious rapture. They do not look inward toward a merely personal interiority. They are not fixed straight ahead, awaiting the leader's signal. They are turned toward a central point: the responsibility of each individual is engaged, and of all those who meet one another's eyes. The promise of happiness (beauty, in Bach's music) is on a different plane—the work, of course, is entitled *Requiem*, an acknowledgement perhaps of the difficulty....

Jaar's work aspires to visibilize, to bring out needs that are now obscurely sensed, that now ache and unsettle us as though they were a phantom limb of the social body. It aspires to visibilize what is obscured by a "a vast, stifling denial in the public realm"[51] for a society dazzled by a level of image overload that exceeds our capacity to respond to what is shown. In his case, this public realm encompasses the whole world: something that Chileans, with their traditional insularity, can perhaps grasp only by a major effort of the imagination—an effort that cannot be shirked, in any case, in our present times.

It is the poetic force in Jaar's work that aspires to make this visibilization tremble on the very verge of its possible realization and thus "irradiate,"[52] become "radiant." It is what provides not just verbal information but visual experiences which coax and even compel us to "unframe" ourselves, to put the mental habits of modern thought ("cages," Max Weber called them) to the test,[53] to go outside ourselves, to let ourselves be carried away, and finally to be moved, to feel the force of Rilke's admonition: "You must change your life." The artist has often referred to the enormity of the task he has set himself, the difficulty and even the impossibility of thinking in these utopian terms in the present day. Yet he does not give up the attempt. In his most recent work, *Muxima*, the utopian dream may be that of a heart that does not exist yet: a heart being born out of music—music as breath, as spirit, as a catalyst for a human community that exists only in desire—and in the recognizable fragments that the artist stages for us, the viewers.

¹ The word "poetics" is used here in its broadest possible sense, deriving from its etymological origin in *poiesis*: to produce, "make," "give form": a set of principles or rules, explicit or not, conscious or unconscious, followed by an artist, an author, a craftsman… "In this broad original sense of the word, every art—not only the verbal kind—is poetry, pro-duction into presence…" (Giorgio Agamben, *The Man without Content*, Stanford, Stanford University Press, 1999, originally published in Italian in 1970).

² "Conversations," in the present volume.

³ In *Behind the Times: The Decline and Fall of the Twentieth-Century Avant Gardes*, London, Thames & Hudson, 1998, Eric Hobsbawm argues that the history of the visual arts in the twentieth century is that of "the struggle against technological obsolescence" (p.12) and their inability to survive the competition from new technical media that were much better able to express the century in which they had arisen (p.27). Jaar's work does not look as though it will be condemned to technological obsolescence.

⁴ James Baldwin, quoted in the epigraph to Alfredo Jaar's book *The Fire This Time: Public Interventions 1979-2005*, Milan, Charta, 2005.

⁵ Xavier Rubert de Ventós, *El arte ensimismado*, Barcelona, Anagrama, 1996.

⁶ Eric Hobsbawm, *op. cit.*, p.32.

⁷ Cf. Jürgen Habermas, "Modernity: An Unfinished Project," in *Habermas and the Unfinished Project of Modernity: Critical Essays on the Philosophical Discourse of Modernity*, Cambridge, Massachusetts, The MIT Press, 1997.

⁸ Jacques Rancière, *El viraje ético de la estética y de la política*, Santiago, Palinodia, 2005, p.48.

⁹ Alfredo Jaar, *A Hundred Times Nguyen*, Stockholm, Fotografiska Museet and Moderna Museet, 1994. Something similar might be said about the visibilization in *The Eyes of Gutete Emerita* and *The Silence of Nduwayezu*, whose visualization—or "staging," as the artist has also expressed it—is wholly different. Cf. Bruno Cuneo's essay in this volume.

¹⁰ T.S. Eliot, "Hamlet and His Problems," in *Selected Essays*, London, Faber & Faber, 1934, p.145.

¹¹ Interview with Anne-Marie Ninacs, in *Le souci du document: Le mois de la photo à Montréal, 1999*, Vox, Montreal, 1999.

¹² *Ibid.*

¹³ Judith Butler, *Undoing Gender*, New York and London, Routledge, 2004: "The Hegelian tradition links desire with recognition, claiming that desire is always the desire for recognition and that it is only through the experience of recognition that any of us becomes constituted as a socially viable being," p.2.

¹⁴ See, in this volume, the essays by Pablo Chiuminatto—particularly what he has to say about respect—and Bruno Cuneo, who refers to "devotion."

¹⁵ "Politics is imagination or else it is a treadmill… disintegrative, stifling, finally brutalizing—or ineffectual." Adrienne Rich, "The Muralist," in *What is Found There: Notebooks on Poetry and Politics*, New York/London, W.W. Norton & Company, 1994, p.49.

¹⁶ "Conversations," in the present volume.

¹⁷ Judith Butler, *op. cit.*

¹⁸ In Chile we well remember the distinction between "humans" and "humanoids" publicly drawn by Admiral José Toribio Merino, a member of the military junta.

¹⁹ See Bruno Cuneo's contribution in this volume.

²⁰ I owe this expression to a remarkable book of Guy Brett's, *Carnival of Perception: Selected Writings on Art*, London, Institute of International Visual Arts (inIVA), 2004, p.13.

²¹ Judith Butler, *op. cit.*, p.15, referring to Freud's text *Instinct and its Vicissitudes*.

²² Rainer Maria Rilke, "Torso of an Archaic Apollo," in *Rilke: Selected Poems*, Berkeley, University of California Press, 1957, trans. C.F. MacIntyre.

²³ Jeremy Gilbert-Rolfe, *Beauty and the Contemporary Sublime*, New York, Allworth Press, 1999. Cf. also *Uncontrollable Beauty: Toward a New Aesthetics*, Bill Beckley (ed.) with David Shapiro, New York, Allworth Press, 1998.

²⁴ See Sandra Accatino's contribution in this volume, where beauty is also referred to very perceptively as a "bait."

²⁵ Arthur C. Danto, *The Abuse of Beauty: Aesthetics and the Concept of Art*, Peru, Illinois, Open Court Publishing Company, 2003, p.139.

²⁶ See Rodrigo Zúñiga's contribution in the present volume.

²⁷ See Ana María Risco's contribution in the present volume.

²⁸ *It Is Difficult*, Toronto, Canada, 1997.

²⁹ In the "Conversations" included in this volume.

³⁰ Arthur C. Danto, *op. cit.*, p.133.

³¹ Adriana Valdés, in *Composición de lugar: Escritos sobre cultura*, Santiago, Universitaria, 1996.

³² Adrienne Rich, *op. cit.*, p.162.

³³ In the "Conversations" already cited.

³⁴ The expression is taken from Jeff Derksen and Neil Smith's text "A Geography of the Difficult," in *Alfredo Jaar*, Rome, MACRO (Museo d'Arte Contemporanea), 2005, p.68. Cf. Sandra Accatino's contribution in the present volume for a description and a more thorough analysis of the work.

³⁵ These terms are taken from Guy Debord and Gilles Deleuze, respectively.

³⁶ "A guilty victim, choosing mistakes," as the artist has put it.

³⁷ From the "Conversations" in the present volume.

³⁸ See Michael Corris, "White Out," on Alfredo Jaar's lament for lost images, *Art Monthly*, London, The Arts Council of England, October 2002, no. 260, pp.6-10.

³⁹ Ticio Escobar, citing Mario Perniola, in *El arte fuera de sí*, Asunción, Paraguay, Fondec/Museo del Barro, 2004, p.202.

⁴⁰ Michael Corris, *op. cit.*

⁴¹ *Requiem for Leipzig*, 2005.

⁴² The expression is Jean-Luc Nancy's. See his work *The Inoperative Community*, Minneapolis/London, University of Minnesota Press, 1991, trans. Peter Connor and Lisa Garbus.

⁴³ Adrienne Rich, *op. cit.*, p. 215.

⁴⁴ From the "Conversations" in this volume.

⁴⁵ *The Gramsci Trilogy* consists of a prologue, three works and an epilogue. The present exhibition includes the prologue, *Searching for Gramsci*; the first part, *Infinite Cell*, and the second part, *Let One Hundred Flowers Bloom*. The other two works are *The Ashes of Gramsci* (exhibited in Rome in 2005) and *The Aesthetics of Resistance*, a public intervention in Como.

⁴⁶ Concerning *The Gramsci Trilogy*, see Pablo Chiuminatto's essay in this book.

⁴⁷ The reference is to Gramsci's "organic intellectual."

⁴⁸ For fuller consideration of *Muxima* that is less restricted to the subject of poetics, I refer the reader to my text on the work in the present volume.

⁴⁹ Giorgio Agamben, *Profanazioni*, Rome, Nottetempo, 2005, citing Simondon. "To be moved is to feel the impersonal that is within us…"

⁵⁰ "I can reiterate poetry" is a line by the Chilean poet Enrique Lihn.

⁵¹ The phrase is from Adrienne Rich, "A Leak in History," *op. cit.*, p.78.

⁵² Read in Ticio Escobar his considerations on the golden composition, *op. cit.*

⁵³ "No one knows who will live in this cage in the future, or whether at the end of this tremendous development entirely new prophets will arise, or there will be a great rebirth of old ideas and ideals, or, if neither, mechanized petrification embellished with a sort of convulsive self-importance. For the last stage of this cultural development, it might well be truly said: 'Specialists without spirit, sensualists without heart; this nullity imagines that it has obtained a level of civilization never before achieved.'" Max Weber, "Asceticism and the Spirit of Capitalism," in *The Protestant Ethic and the Spirit of Capitalism*, London, Routledge, 1987 (reprint of 1930 edition), trans. Talcott Parsons, p.182.

Alfredo Jaar,
Conversations in Chile 2005

Sandra Accatino

Pablo Chiuminatto

Bruno Cuneo

Ana María Risco

Adriana Valdés

Rodrigo Zúñiga

In November 2005, Alfredo Jaar met with us over two and a half days in Santiago to talk about his work, the exhibition planned for the following year at Fundación Telefónica (Chile), and the book we would be bringing out to accompany that exhibition. These were long, intense discussions between the artist and the people who would be writing the texts in the book: myself, as editorial coordinator, and the other contributors, Sandra Accatino, Pablo Chiuminatto, Bruno Cuneo, Ana María Risco, and Rodrigo Zúñiga, all of them younger writers who have distinguished themselves in the doctorate program at the Faculty of Arts of the University of Chile. We did not originally mean to publish what was said; the discussions were totally uninhibited, and we recorded them mainly as an aid to memory when we should come to write. It was only later, reviewing them together, that we realized parts of this recorded material could be of interest to many of those who would be attending the exhibition. The conversational format was, we thought, very accessible for a general readership and for those new to Alfredo Jaar's work.

What follows are extracts from these long conversations, the preference being given to the artist's own words. The tone is very colloquial and relaxed, even humorous at times. The rest of us have had our say in the essays of this book and so, when these conversations were transcribed, it was Alfredo Jaar's voice, its immediacy, what he had to tell us about his work, its relationship to Chile, and the state of contemporary art, that we really wanted to transmit.

A.V.

THE LOGIC OF THIS EXHIBITION

Alfredo Jaar About the choice of works to be shown in Santiago. Ideally I would have shown only new works, but it wasn't possible; I did want to include my latest work, though, *Muxima*, which will be shown for the first time in February 2006, in New York. The second thing I couldn't leave out was *Lament of the Images*, because it was in the news here recently, and because it's right at the center of my thinking about images, photography, and the inability to see. Then, I had just finished my work on Gramsci, and I still had the idea of showing things that were as recent as possible. But what with the prologue and epilogue, the *Gramsci Trilogy* is really five works, and that's a lot, too much. So I left out the last one, the projection on to the Casa del Fascio in Como, because it was too specific to Italy—although fascism is in the air everywhere these days. The fourth one, *The Ashes of Gramsci*, is a beautiful piece I did for a gallery in Rome, but it didn't fit with what I wanted to do here. Of the trilogy, *Infinite Cell* and *Let One Hundred Flowers Bloom* were the strongest, the ones that meant the most here. Because of the almost impossible struggle of intellectuals, and because they reflect the horrors we're caught up in today. So those two Gramsci works went in, and that made four. There was only room for four more. That was a dilemma. I thought of *A Logo for America* because it's the work of mine that's been reproduced the most, a public intervention that put me on the map. It's very early, too, from '87. And it connects to Chile, to Latin America... Three to go. The logic then was: I've worked a lot in Africa, the Rwanda project is crucial to my work, twenty pieces created over six years. I thought of *Real Pictures*, *The Eyes of Gutete Emerita*, five or six possibilities. I finally decided on *The Silence of Nduwayezu*, because *The Eyes...* has been seen the most, and *The Silence...* is equivalent and uses the same formal strategy. That left the obvious: to round off with one work based on Asia and one based on Latin America. *Out of Balance*, about Latin America, from the 1980s, makes an interesting connection, a short circuit, with *Lament of the Images*. From Asia there were several, but I made my name in the 1980s with lightboxes combined with mirrors, and there wasn't any work like that in the show. So I decided on *Untitled (water)*. And that made eight.

Afterwards I decided that *Searching for Gramsci*, the prologue, could go in the first room at the Galería Gabriela Mistral, before reaching *Let One Hundred Flowers Bloom*. So ultimately, three parts of the Gramsci Trilogy will be shown: the prologue, *Searching for Gramsci*; the first part, *Infinite Cell*; and the second part, *Let One Hundred Flowers Bloom*.

A WORK FOR CHILE

Pablo Chiuminatto There are no works made for Chile in this show. But you must have thought about what it would mean to show these works in this country...

AJ Ideally we would have included a work created specially for Chile. But I wasn't up to it...

Ana María Risco When you say you weren't up to it... you couldn't manage it in time? What's the complicating factor?

AJ For fifteen years we have been trying to do an exhibition of my work in Chile, and nothing came of it for various reasons, financing, organization. Now finally, thanks to the support from Fundación Telefónica Chile, I'll be able to give an overview of what I've been doing in the 25 years since I left. It's not a retrospective, just an overview of my work.

The ideal would have been to include a new, unseen work created especially for Chile. I decided against it, for reasons of stress. I've shown all around the world, but coming to Chile makes me nervous, because what I went through here was very tough, tough enough to make me leave. I went through quite a lot.

I'm sure there would have been some who would have said that it's twenty-five years since I left, and the first thing I do when I'm back is make a work about Chile, for Chile: I wanted to avoid that problem. It seemed wiser, as a first stage in my return, to show works I've done abroad. It seemed more appropriate to create a Chile-specific work next time, if there is a next time.

But, quite honestly, I didn't have the time either. We had less than one year from when the contract was signed, and I've never created a new work in less than a year. I've got some material on Chile which I think is excellent, and which I'm keeping back for now, a project I'm thinking over. But doing it in such a short time, and in those circumstances, would have been as stressful as the other eight works I'm showing combined.

Sandra Accatino But now they're going to say that you are Chilean and you've done nothing for Chile...

AJ I'm doomed either way...

Bruno Cuneo Hand out *copihues*[1] at the entrance...

(*Laughter*)

WHAT MIGHT HAVE BEEN

SA There was a work in Chile that appeared in the catalog of public interventions you've just published, but wasn't carried out in the end. Wasn't it the one for the Ministry of Education?

AJ Yes, it was specific to that place, the entrance lobby of the Ministry, in the Alameda. My idea was to make a gigantic lightbox. And then via the Internet, connected to hospitals, I had worked with some MIT engineers to come up with a system so that the lightbox would light up every time a child was born in Chile, with a system of colors specific to each child. The colors were going to appear along with the time of birth and the name. And then it would go out again until the next birth.

AMR A bit like the work involving the homeless, in Canada. [2]

AJ Yes. It was going to be financed by the Asociación Chilena de Seguridad, [3] but then they said it was too expensive.

PC The work you were going to do in the Ministry of Education was very transgressive.

Adriana Valdés And I think it hits a marvelous note: who can refuse to acknowledge the birth of children? And who can reject that reminder of responsibility?

PC A reminder of the time—the one and only time in societies as unequal as ours —when children are equal among themselves...

CHILE, 1979-1981: THE STUDIES ON HAPPINESS [AND AFTER]
THE WORK AND ITS CONTEXT

BC I thought you would include something from the *Studies on Happiness* in this exhibition. What you did then was seminal, I think. In that work, something that begins as a question about happiness ends up as a kind of anatomy of all possible forms of unhappiness. I think that initial question is always there in your work, anyway, even if your skepticism just keeps growing...

PC In my text on the *Gramsci Trilogy* I make a link with the *Studies on Happiness*. I wonder, if the question was about happiness then, what the question would be now. What is it that we haven't asked ourselves about now?

AV The funny thing is that at the time the question was seen here as naïve and not the kind of thing you were supposed to think politically. Only with the return of democracy, in 1989, did people start talking in political and sociological terms about the subject of happiness.

BC "Are you happy?" is the ultimate political question... Perhaps people were blinded in a way, just because the question was so rhetorically effective in that context—which is paradoxical, of course.

PC The narrative then was always about action, grieving. What the work does, instead of asking you to denounce something, is to ask you to proclaim something, and that confused people... Everyone was speaking the same language, it was two sides of one coin, about authority and about power... You took the position of an onlooker who is able to articulate the question from a different angle.

SA People might have felt that the question "Are you happy?" was very aggressive.

BC Semantic impertinence to the power of three...

Rodrigo Zúñiga I think, with hindsight, that it hit a note of humor in a context where that just wasn't possible.

AJ It's humorous at a distance.

RZ Some of the answers from the public are very cogent, and the questions were difficult to answer.

PC Do you remember that phrase: "How are you?" "I'm fine, but I'll get over it." (*Laughter*)

AJ I approached that work as an architect, setting myself a program. I wanted to explore the limits of what could be done, as poetically as possible. I remember that censorship was at its height, and worse than that, self-censorship, because people were scared. I wanted to play with that: what could be said, how far you could take it, and what the most poetical way of doing it was. Something almost watertight. I was reading Bergson at the time, his studies on laughter, which I liked a lot, and that's what led me to "studies on happiness." I thought: "it's watertight, it's poetic, it's naïve; they're not going to do anything to me." So then I decided on the program of seven interventions and got to work. I was very isolated in the art world.

BC And yet, Alfredo, the nearest thing to what you did in Chile was the work of the Colectivo Acciones de Arte (CADA). I mean that determination to get out of the museum and use the urban fabric as the basis for a "social sculpture," a concept they took from Beuys and Fluxus [4]... Their work was multifaceted too, with poetry and video... The funny thing is that they got a lot of recognition at the time, and rightly so, but you didn't.

AV Repression was everywhere in public life then, of course, what with the lack of civic freedoms, and throughout education, even university art teaching—that wasn't just restricted, there was very little of it. But even where there was cultural resistance, in the movement of intellectual and artistic dissidence that came to be called the "escena de avanzada," there was exclusion and authoritarianism too, an orthodoxy that was becoming stifling in those years, as Enrique Lihn pointed out later. In Alfredo's case, people were just not capable of seeing his work, appreciating what he was trying to do—even though, as Bruno says, CADA did achieve recognition.

I wanted to write about this work of Alfredo's precisely because it was beyond me at the time, beyond what I was capable of thinking and writing. For example, it was necessary to deal with the world of communications; and that wasn't recognized here as a subject for theory until some time afterwards. Sometimes things don't get through just because people lack the tools for reading them… because there are blind spots, places that are not on their mental map.

PC Talking about blind spots, do you remember what Buchloh says in the prologue to his book about not seeing the work of women artists? He reproaches himself for it. I didn't see it, he says. There they were, and I'm not going to start talking about this now, because I didn't see it at the time.[5]

AJ And the greatest irony is that he lived with a woman artist, Louise Lawler…

AV And then with Cathy De Zegher, who dedicated a lot of time to women's art.

PC When you were here in the 1980s, what contexts were you aware of? When you did the *Studies on Happiness*, did you know Hans Haacke's work, for instance?

AJ Yes, I knew it very well. I started in 1979, and the project culminated in 1981.

RZ The thing about the surveys was partly a citation from Haacke, wasn't it, or did it come from somewhere else?

AJ At that time I was citing Haacke. Ironically, I found out later that Haacke was citing David Lamelas, an Argentine, who still hasn't been given his due in the art scene. People didn't see any further than Haacke. I know David: his work is only now starting to get more recognition in Europe.[6]

RZ What happened to the tapes you made for that project?

AJ I have them all. Hundreds and hundreds of hours. And I don't know what to do with them.

PC I wonder where the people you taped are now? What's become of them? Some very odd Chilean stories could be recovered by following the thread of the filming in the street… Stick them together chronologically, a bit like *Russian Ark*, it would be amazing… Wouldn't it be something to try and find out who they are, the other side of the camera. What would they say now if you asked them: so what about it, were you happy then, are you happy now?

AMR Patricio Guzmán did a follow-up like that, when he brought characters from *La batalla de Chile* back together[7]…

OUTS AND INS

RZ Despite all this, you did put together the *IN/OUT* exhibition with other Chilean artists, and there was another one in Buenos Aires where you were with them...[8]

AJ It occurred to me to do something with the Washington Project for the Arts (WPA), which was a great institution then. I'd met the director, Al Nodal, through Ana Mendieta, and I suggested an exhibition of Chilean artists. He agreed and I suggested Dittborn, Downey, and CADA; two of us were outs and two were ins. It took on a life of its own; invitations were sent out, and everyone did their own thing. Not long after, the CAYC in Buenos Aires started planning an exhibition. Nelly Richard invited Gonzalo Díaz, CADA, Leppe, and Dittborn. She only included me because the director of the CAYC, Jorge Glusberg, said to—he was interested in my work. Not a very nice way to be invited, but I only found out afterwards. I was left out of *Margins and Institutions*,[9] Nelly Richard's book about art in Chile, and that wasn't very nice either. She said there wasn't enough information, but I think there was. Actually, looking back, it was the best thing that could have happened to me.

AV You avoided becoming dependent in any way. And the splits that followed.

BC *Studies on Happiness* seems to be your most easily classifiable work. It's the only work of yours included in Osborne's book on conceptual art.[10]

AJ They haven't been able to pigeonhole the rest. There's no label that fits it. There's nowhere to put me.

BC Is "conceptual artist" a term that applies to you?

AV Conceptual art has been relegated to the 1970s, neo-conceptualism is the term now.

AJ I love the idea of working with ideas, and obviously that's what I do; but the end result doesn't seem to fit the definitions. It falls into another category. I just don't care.

NEW YORK IN THE 1980S
A LOGO FOR AMERICA

AJ When I began to study the New York art world, I found it was very inward-looking. The outside world didn't exist there, as far as I could see. It was almost a fictional world people were living in. I had a weird ambition: I wanted to bring a bit of reality into that world. The question was how to do it in a way that didn't just repeat stereotypes, or turn me into part of that fiction. That was the starting point for the program I set myself. As you know, I didn't study art: I come from the world of architecture. What I do as an architect is set myself a program, and that was my program then.

About *A Logo for America*, which has been reproduced more than almost any of my works... In 1987 I had an invitation from an organization called the Public Art Fund, which meant I had the opportunity to show something for sixty seconds every six minutes in Times Square. For the exhibition here we're going to use the documentation on what happened in '87. We're actually going to screen advertisements before and after, to show the context. It was a very privileged, very visible site. It made Jenny Holzer famous.

RZ It's one of the most violent and direct of all your works... To come back to Jenny Holzer, with that kind of short-circuiting of stereotypes... Your idea was to bring up another problem of exclusion. And isn't there a connection with Magritte?

AJ Yes, *This Is Not a Pipe*... This is not America. The thing was to really push it, be quite explicit. That work was a reaction to the way the word America has been usurped by the United States, and we've been wiped off the map. And it's become a worldwide problem. Europeans also talk about America, or l'*Amérique*, when they just mean the United States. It was a subversive gesture—not that it made a difference, of course.

RZ Pound said that social conflicts were conflicts of language...

AJ The work was clear, direct, didactic, with very specific objectives. What I'm proudest of is that it's in about 18 school text books in the United States. It's used by teachers of multiculturalism, of identity... I felt I was part of a movement, there was something there. Not exactly a community of artists, but friendships. We were all unknowns at the time.

RZ That work is a very effective example of how to act outside the art scene.

AJ It was about using creativity and a public space to speak out against a false, negative image of our continent. It was the first animation I did, almost a miniature film. The most spectacular reaction came from NPR (National Public Radio), which went to Times Square and asked people what they thought. There were people who said it was against the law...

LESSONS IN GEOPOLITICS

RZ About the intervention in *Flash Art* magazine, in 1998. How was that arranged?

AJ I was invited to do an intervention in the magazine. And my intervention was to create a new index for *Flash Art*. I wanted to put it at the beginning, as though it were the real index, but they wouldn't let me.

SA You were trying to suggest another possible editorial line for the magazine, to show there were other subjects out there apart from what the magazine included...

AJ And to give visibility to authors who lacked it in publications like that at the time. Like Raúl Ruiz, Glauber Rocha, Cildo Meireles, for example.

AV That's also what you did later on, I think, with your *Emergency* project. In that work, Africa emerges very slowly, for a few moments, from an expanse of dark water—and then disappears again. In the book of that name, what you did was to give visibility to twenty-five writers of African origin. You used your position to create a position of visibility for others. At least, that was how I read it... With *Flash Art* you brought together a quantity of names, sometimes with no apparent relationship between them. What was the affinity you wanted to show?

AJ They were people I admired, that's all, who had no visibility in that milieu, they were invisible.

Various What happened then was like a Borges story (*laughter*). Now almost all of them are there: Homi Bhabha, Gayatri Spivak, Gerardo Mosquera...

RZ How did you arrange it?

AJ I don't arrange things, I get invited. When I arrived in New York, dispatched by this woman here [11]—"off with you," she said—I was very organized, with slides of my work in Chile, including *Studies on Happiness*. I took six months or so to choose the ten galleries I liked best. I made up ten packages of material about my work, beautifully organized, and I delivered them to these galleries. First I waited a couple of weeks, nothing. Then a month went by. Nothing. Then I decided to go and see what was going on. What happened to me then was definitely the biggest humiliation of my life, and it really left its mark on me. Five envelopes were never opened. Three were opened, but only to insert a standard letter saying thanks but no thanks. The other two were opened right there in front of me by the gallery receptionists; they looked at the slides and said "no, thank you." That was when I made myself a promise: I was never going to approach anyone again. They would have to approach me. I was earning my living as an architect at the time. And I really never have approached anyone again. What happened was a real shower of cold water, a lesson about the geopolitics of the art world. Naively, I delivered texts in Spanish... I was from Chile... Today's multiculturalism was a far-off dream then, a utopia. But it was the best thing that could have happened to me, learning that lesson.

RZ When were you first approached?

AJ I was working as an architect at SITE, and someone there who knew I was an artist invited me to an exhibition. One thing led to another—that was in 1982.

PUBLIC VENUES AND ART VENUES

AMR I'd like to know what you see as being the differences between your work in public venues and in art venues.

AJ They're totally different. I do public interventions because I need to get out of the perfect white cube, the art world, which I see as pretty fictitious. Public interventions happen in the real world, and they keep me real.

AV You run a risk…

AJ You can design them down to the last detail, but in public spaces anything can happen. In art venues, everything works the way you intended.

AMR But in the neat white cube there's time to stop and look, an atmosphere…

AJ It's not to be looked down on. Even though you're preaching to the converted. You need to use every space available, public or private.

AMR Are you attracted more by public spaces?

AJ No, what attracts me are problems… A problem in a private venue can sometimes be very interesting.

AV There's more of an interdisciplinary feel to public spaces, where you can't control the reaction you'll get: you come up against every possible way of thinking. To reach the public in open spaces like that you're more or less forced to work with what's out there in the real world—or rather, the world outside of art (I'm not too sure about that word "real").

AMR I'm interested by what you say about where your work fits in, the difficulty of placing it on a particular disciplinary level. It seems to have a kind of freedom of movement: I think that's very good for art.

ART HISTORY: ANY CONNECTION?

AMR Your work connects to very contemporary visual practices, including advertising. How does it relate to the history of art? Are there citations, critiques, how does it work?

AJ I'm almost tempted to say there's no connection at all. Never having studied art, and studying architecture instead, left me with this incredible freedom. I always said: I'm going to solve this problem, how do I go about it. I'm not tied to any specific material or medium. It was Duchamp who made me take up art: I was just so amazed by the idea that I or anyone could decide what art was. That was the revolution of the twentieth century. Duchamp freed me. His work's got nothing to do with mine…

but he gave me my freedom. That's as revolutionary as you can get. Art is whatever we decide it is. Whether it's good or bad is another matter.

AMR I was thinking of formal references from the artistic tradition...

AJ There are some references in my work. For instance, I work with very minimalist forms. In the 1960s, which were a time of great geopolitical struggles, minimalist forms ignored all that. Mine brought back the information which had been left out. Sometimes, for fun, I use references to some artist I like, Beuys, On Kawara... but it's not something I do consistently.

RZ What do you like about Kawara's work?

AJ The obsessiveness. Completely crazed.

RZ And he's got that veiled quality... the way he circled conceptualism, didn't connect with his peers, his work with dates...

AJ I love the way he creates his own system, his own laws. "Today I'm going to paint a date." 12-20-2005. He decides on the typography and the color. If he doesn't finish it within twenty-four hours he destroys it. And then he puts it in a box with that day's *New York Times*. I just found it amazing that the art world accepted that invention. Now he's an established presence in that world.

BC In the postcards you sent from Rwanda, the first work in the project,[12] some people have seen an allusion to a work of On Kawara's... Anyway, I think your work is inspired much more by the cinema (Antonioni, for example, or Godard) or by poetry than by the visual arts.

RZ I see Alfredo's work as being like Bob Dylan's with poetry: working from the outside, but very refreshing at the same time, very inspiring for those on the inside. Always keeping just clear of anything to do with the mainstream... There's not much point asking about other artists, because you've set out (not necessarily deliberately) to work outside the system of rules. I find that interesting in relation to your educational work: how you transmit that freedom in a context where you would have thought there couldn't be any rules any more, but where people still do follow certain rules.

TEACHING ART

AV Studying architecture saved you from studying art. From what you've been saying, an art education doesn't seem so much an advantage as something that holds you back, especially in repressive or very professionally oriented situations: there's a leveling effect.

PC It's all structured around technique... However much the field may have expanded, that's where it starts. Whereas architecture is a sort of epistemological model, it's about constituting a world.

AV Where the students are concerned, the question of how "problem-solving" can be incorporated into teaching... That's what you showed in "Art and Politics"...

SA Is art something that can be taught at a university?

AJ I give a third of my time to exhibitions, a third to public interventions, and a third to teaching. To my mind, each third has the same importance... I hold five or six intensive seminars a year. What I tell students is "stop doing things, start thinking." Then we try to create a model for learning to think, for solving a problem.

BC For example?

AJ The last seminar I did, in the Canary Islands, just a week ago. It was attended by philosophers, artists, choreographers, dancers, sculptors, painters, an engraver, an engineer... We sat down and talked. We took a week to decide what subject they were interested in, until they came to the conclusion that culture in the Canary Islands was dying. Institutions have been shut down, cultural funding has been cut, magazines have closed... There are a lot of competitions in Spain, but it costs artists from the Canary Islands a fortune to send their work there. We designed a project called "The Canaries: Can culture die?" They decided to work as a group. In the middle of the second week, they came up with the idea of creating an altar to the Canary Islands culture that is dying. We started off doing different exercises, until they decided to work with candles... They filmed candles going out, and each of the students read a text on culture in the Canaries, and as they each read their lament the candles would be going out, one after another... The final installation was ten video projections, with ten candles at different stages of extinction, and you heard all ten voices at the same time, lamenting the state of culture in the Canaries. The piece was subtitled so you could follow it visually as well. It's still being shown. And the press picked up on everything.

NEW YORK: THE STUDIO AND PROJECT MANAGEMENT

AJ In my studio we keep flow charts of the projects I'm working on. Each project has its phases. Ideally they should never coincide, either at the start or when they come to be shown. I have a studio manager who coordinates everything; I usually install a project only the first time round, when it hasn't been shown before. Another assistant works with the pictures, the animations, and the web. I also work with a cameraman who filmed with me in Angola and takes care of the technical side. Another assistant is a sort of intern, he deals with more basic stuff and support. The studio is a laboratory of creation, it's for thinking and creating, like an architecture studio: not much is produced there, we have things made to order.

RZ How do you go about a project like the Ministry of Education one?

AJ We found some MIT scientists who developed the software for us. I'm a believer in the power of ideas. For me, 90% of the problem is to get at the idea that's going to be the essence of the project. No technical or domestic or administrative problem will stand in my way. We always find the people to do it. I have a project that waited ten years to become technically feasible: it opens in March 2006, in Houston (*The Sound of Silence*, conceived in 1995). We usually organize local support groups for works in situ. Sometimes I create more personal, more private works; others are much more of a collective effort: it depends on the project.

PC And the photographs displayed in the galleries, are they part of the project?

AJ Those are works on a different scale that circulate more easily, and that people can buy. They partially finance my larger, more complex works, which are trickier to sell. In time they are bought by big institutions, but it's not quick. Some are on display in the museums that have bought them...

PC It's a way of going about things that's rather like a baroque workshop, because of the division of functions. And baroque art was political, too.

"I'M A GREAT BELIEVER IN THE ACCUMULATION OF STIMULI"

RZ How do you see your work linking up with cultural producers? How does it open up to this possible dialogue with intellectuals? There are moments in your work when you've taken up this dialogue, especially in the *Gramsci Trilogy*.

AJ It's the first time I've focused so specifically on someone. The other thing, cultural production, is always there in a way, because I'm a big reader, I read all sorts of stuff, but my work with that is not deliberate. I don't wake up and say, I'm going to start with Benjamin, for example. But I do accumulate information. I'm a great believer in the accumulation of stimuli. Sometimes very odd, conflicting ones, in parallel, while I'm creating a project. It's a way of stimulating creativity. I do it with myself but also with my students. You work with things, they suddenly click and then, surprisingly almost, something emerges.

In Italy, for instance, when I was starting to think about a possible work, I was going around Rome and I saw water flowing, always the same watercourses, but divided into a lot of channels: and this very simple image had its symbolism there, which I decided to work with. A new bridge had been built, but part of the old one had been left. I found all this very metaphorical. Mentally, I was inventing new bridges, new connections, in a country that was totally divided, for and against Berlusconi. That same day there was an extraordinary demonstration in Rome against the war in Iraq. Then I arrived at the hotel, and there was a documentary on television about Aimé Césaire, who was the mayor of Fort-de-France in Martinique when I was living there for ten years... So out of all this, something suddenly emerges...

RZ Bruno was talking about your "elective affinities." Do you have favorite authors? Like the way one has tastes in music, for example... Theoretical tastes? Philosophical ones? From what you've just said, Gramsci isn't really one of them. Are you a regular reader?

AJ Yes, I'm very curious, I read a lot. I don't stick to just one field. I think you need to get stimulation from different things, not always be bathing in the same pool, if you follow me.

BC Or with the same water.

AJ But there is one author I come back to again and again: Cioran, who's also non-establishment. He's insane. But I find him restful.

AV What you like, I see, is the potential for a clash: because that shifts your orbit. And it makes constellations of things that wouldn't appear without that clash of very different stimuli, many of them from poetry. On your own web site there is a kind of map of these references. In relation to the work you gave me, *October-Obsolete*: what type of writing about art interests you now? That obviously doesn't...

AJ Not many people interest me. I'm interested in other kinds of writing. I'm more interested in reading about politics, or culture in general, or photography...

AMR People from different backgrounds, with other outlooks...

RZ Do you read art magazines?

AJ I read some magazines regularly, like *Art Monthly*, *New Left Review*, *Domus*,

Cahiers du Cinéma, London Review of Books, others on technology and music. I also receive *Artforum* and *Art in America*, but I just skim them. I try to keep abreast, but art magazines have gone terribly downhill. Because of the advertising...

SA And the quality of what they show is poor...

PC Why do you think the visual arts are where they are?

AJ The market dominates—things really have changed amazingly. The universities, for instance. I've been going to universities for fifteen years. Young people used to be experimental and uncommercial. Now they're thinking about exhibiting before they've left the university. The galleries send people to the year-end exhibitions and choose their artists. And that helps the universities to sell their courses. Before it was all about intellectual prestige, experimentation, famous artists... Now it's the market. Everything's inflated. The fairs have a new presence. Ten years ago, artists hated them. Now they've become a draw, they're glamorous. You're asked to produce works specially for fairs. Basel, London, Miami/Basel, ARCO, etc. This is new. People buy and buy... The auction system distorts everything. People pay crazy prices, but they know that in a year's time they'll get more. It's almost Hollywood.

AV The sales statistics of Sotheby's and Christie's mean that works are quoted by transaction volume and price, like stock market securities. I told you about the conference on investing in art that was given here in Santiago by an economist, Sebastián Edwards, at the Centro de Estudios Públicos (CEP).

AJ I don't want to see my works in those places, but it's inevitable. They're changed totally there. I've got a system: if anyone has a work of mine and wants to sell it, I always offer them the amount they paid plus 10%, and that way I sometimes get them back.

RZ What's your relationship with curators? Do you have power issues with them?

AJ Most of the people I've worked with have been very generous: I propose how my works are going to be shown. There are problems with the architecture of museums, though. There are architects who think they're artists, and they create architectural spaces that are impossible for art, like Gehry. Really they're creating sculptures in their own honor. There are others, like Renzo Piano, who create respectful, clean, quiet places an artist can work in.

BC Young artists in Chile don't know how to mount exhibitions. The venues are depressing. And again, poets publish books that are very sloppy in terms of design. This concept, which is so important in your work, doesn't seem to exist here. Any publicist can do things much better... and that's serious.

TWO INSTALLATIONS: *OUT OF BALANCE* AND *UNTITLED (WATER)*

AJ To come back to New York, the impression it made on me when I arrived there. As I say, I saw it was an insular world, an ivory tower; I thought it was so privileged that it was becoming unreal. So I decided to travel, precisely to bring in something from outside, from a different world. My first major project was on Serra Pelada, the mines in Brazil. With that I was trying to ask, in New York, what world are you living in? I was trying to show someone else's reality, a different world.

It may sound naïve, but I think that for all its failings, the world of art and culture is still the only one where something like that can be done... The media can't do it any more; they've become a vulgar business like any other. The world of culture—museums and universities—is the last place where you are still free to dream of a better world...

It's an extraordinary opportunity we have, because society still leaves this space for arguing and inventing (although the pressure to control it is increasing all the time). I find it so natural to do it there. I wouldn't know what else to do. I don't know if it's because of my training, but I've not been able to create a single work of art that isn't a response to something real. I can't do it. I'm a project artist, not a studio artist. I'm always surprised to see how other artists can create something out of nothing... It's true that in the world of art you really can think very subversively. Now, whether that actually affects reality is a different matter. At least we can offer models, take a utopian view.

I wanted to find a way to get viewers to commit themselves physically and so to make, metaphorically, that initial commitment, before taking it further and going on to involve themselves in some other way. The context for achieving this was the installation, and that's what I started with.

In the works on the Serra Pelada miners, *Rushes* and *Out of Balance*, I wanted to capture the human being. Take human beings out of the context that exoticized them. My idea was that to see *Out of Balance* people would have to physically balance, because the work is visually tilted to the side. This balancing effort is, metaphorically, a way of envisioning a new balance in society. I am forcing the viewer to make that intellectual effort. Then I started to unbalance the spaces themselves: a negative within a negative makes a positive. That's what I wanted to suggest.

AV And that way you disrupt the first scene of art, which is contemplation. The contemplative attitude, the distance it involves, is no longer the right one, it's not what's needed...

AMR Viewers are asked to expose their bodies: they are required to physically enter the work.

PC This commitment of the body: unlike traditional contemplation of art, this physical engagement is a way of reviving the concept of the (involuntary) witness. It transforms the viewer into a new class of viewer.

AV Who's more dangerously situated.

SA What's more, the installations don't give up all their information at once. Viewers are prevented from completely satisfying their curiosity and are forced to linger, take their time.

AJ At the time of *Untitled (water)*, I wanted to attract viewers, draw them in so that they would come up close and see the horror, and see themselves as well. They see themselves and then they encounter another person. A lot of people look and think the pictures are inside the wall; they don't realize they're mirrors. And what you see depends on how you move. I'd been using lightboxes and mirrors for almost ten years, but it was the first time that device had occurred to me...

AMR So that people's gaze can move and linger.

AJ And so they know it's fragmented. I can't show everything (the same happens in *Muxima*). I accept fragmentation and I use it. I put these images in your world, but always in a fragmented form, so that my inability to show everything becomes part of the work. As does the dilemma it meant for me to spend several days on the ships that were being used by the immigration authority to track down escaped refugees. It was tricky, because I was with the people who were going to catch them... They were in a concentration camp by that time. I accept my privileged position of having taken the photos, and then I leave. And they're still locked up.

AMR Thinking about *Untitled (water)*, I looked into the subject and traditional migration has been blurring, people are moving from poor countries to less poor ones, wherever they can make a living. And at the same time borders are increasingly closed.

AV For people, not for products. That's been happening in Europe too. Freedom of trade doesn't mean freedom for people.

AMR Closing borders leads to illegal immigration as a matter of course, and it throws up groups of people who exploit the unprotected status of the undocumented to force them into abusive working conditions.

BC That's what makes me suspicious of Negri's hopes for mass global mobility as a microphysics of resistance... [13]

RZ It makes me think of the permanent state of exception that Agamben speaks of in *Homo Sacer*, of refugees whose belonging has been obliterated. What's called "bare life."

AJ In Spain, there's the tragedy of the pateras [14] bringing in African immigrants. When I was in the Canaries, one arrived with fifty-five people in it. Twenty had died. They were all from African countries a long way apart. If you analyze how much they paid to get into that boat... Obviously it's not that they don't have the money, it's that they don't have any legal way of getting into these countries.

RZ It shows how the African continent has been effaced, how it has been left to its fate.

PC Gramsci has a passage about Africa. His utopia was that those who had been taken off as slaves would rebuild the continent. About Chile (and Peru and Argentina too) he says that in the cultural struggle they haven't succeeded in resolving the problem of cultural dependence on the ecclesiastical and military establishment.

THE RWANDA PROJECT: *THE SILENCE OF NDUWAYEZU*

BC After *A Logo for America*, your relationship with your subject-matter starts to come under strain as you seem to develop very deep doubts about the expressive capabilities of the media you work with. I'm thinking, specifically, of your mistrust of the photographic image as an agent of visibility and the way you thematize that mistrust from then on...

AJ Yes, there was a crisis. For the first time I started looking at my work as exercises in representation. In the Rwanda project I thought all my attempts had failed. In the thirteenth project I came up with the format of *The Eyes of Gutete Emerita*, which is the same I used for *The Silence of Nduwayezu*... The work on Gutete was very effective. All sorts of things happened, it made a big impact, and that's why I used the same format for a different story. Gutete's are the eyes that have seen what we refused to see. With Nduwayezu's eyes I was trying to portray silence. They're very grainy, the picture is more blurred. It was one attempt more. Then I despaired again and went off to look for another format.

This project has gone into another world now, not just the world of art. It's difficult, emotionally and psychologically.

PC How many times did you travel to Rwanda?

AJ Twice, for a month in all. My psychiatrist didn't want to let me go again. There were people who went all prepared and they hardly lasted twenty-four hours. It was intolerable.

AV An excess of reality...

BC There's a feeling of powerlessness running right through this work: a kind of acknowledgement of the impossibility of representation.

RZ I have the feeling that in the earlier works there was this suspicion of the role of the image, and that this intensified with Rwanda. In the Rwanda project there is something more than mistrust: there's an almost visceral pulling apart. Something only a witness can feel. The first hesitation, the first tremor. This work on silence is really very important and very powerful in relation to the politics of the image.

SA The questions posed are different as well.

BC There's also an ethical engagement in that work which, unlike the media's work with catastrophe, cries out for political results. I would say that what is being deployed in that work is a "politics of observation," in a context where everything is dominated by sensationalism and stereotyping, if not indifference...

AJ Sometimes I feel like a frustrated reporter. The first thing we have to do is inform, because the media doesn't do it properly, or does it in the crudest way. I sometimes think it would be telling to go out into the street with a camera and ask people what's going on now in Afghanistan, Iraq, Pakistan... People know very little. They get unconnected scraps of information, filtered by ideology. The first thing you have to do in a work is establish a little bit of context. Politically, my first job is to say, "there's this country, there was this genocide, and we didn't do anything, a million people died, this is what we could have done." You might say, "This isn't art." But there are ways and ways of doing it. If I stick to the raw public information, it's not interesting as art. I want to be able to move you, challenge you, touch you. I want to be able to irritate you, provoke you: that's a political task. But it's very hard. How do I work? With information and emotion, information and culture, information and spectacle... The piece you're going to be working with (*The Silence of Nduwayezu*) is the thirteenth in the Rwanda series. I want to show this child's eyes. But that image will very quickly disappear from the public mind. What can I do to keep it there? It has to be spectacular, but make sense too. I'm suggesting: this is what you need to know. And then I offer you this image in the hope that, backed up by this text, it will be very powerful. And that is very hard. And works fail. Because they're either too weighted toward information or toward spectacle... How do you strike such a perfect balance that it's informative, moving, inspires people to think and act... I've no idea how you do it. But that's what we're working on. More political than that...

RZ But despite everything they resolve themselves at a visual level. That's essential. In *The Silence of Nduwayezu*, for instance, there's something calligrammatic: a line... A connection between figure and letter...

PC And there are the corridors. Like a dream world, or like Nerval, the bowels of the city, the corridor as a place of vanished footsteps... Or suspense.

BC Or someone whose strength is failing... The light at the end of the tunnel.

AV Imminence creates desire. It prepares you to see the work. Like with *The Lament of the Images*.

AJ Half the people don't read; but a lot come back, after seeing it, to read the texts... Also, people took away lots of slides—we could see that from the security videos. I gave instructions that this shouldn't be prevented. I was very intrigued by the way people took away the pictures from the Gutete and Nduwayezu works. About a hundred thousand slides have been taken. They're not appealing images; they're very sad. The moment I'm interested in is when the viewer's eyes are an inch away from Nduwayezu's...

SA In an artist's book you used the reflection of people's own eyes where Gutete's were... There's a total jump of identity.

RZ You put me in mind of *Diálogo de ojos*, a work of Lygia Clark's; it's a mechanism you put on, a device, a kind of mask, where you see your own eyes: a virtual mechanism like looking through someone else's eyes.

ARTISTS AND AUTHORITY

AJ We artists are like ants beside the powerful... But we reach a privileged minority, the people who participate in the arts and culture.

AV And then they suddenly start saying that something can no longer be ignored... You can influence a bit, shift the line between what's noticed and what's forgotten for good.

RZ There's also the conditioning power of national politics. You're often asked why you should concern yourself with other places, like the ones in your work, when what most directly affects you is what's happening right here, in your own country. In your work there is this ethical drive to take people's civic awareness, which might be absorbed by their local circumstances, and bring it into a global sphere. The works you did on Nigeria in the 1980s showed how the European and North American way of life was based on this other way of life, on what happened outside their borders.

PC And again, after living in Paris for a year and witnessing how concerned the French were about human rights in "third world" countries, I was really shocked by the total contempt they showed for immigrants in their own city...

AJ In the world of culture, a film—*La haine* (Hatred)—portrayed that situation in Paris. [15] After what's just happened [the serious disturbances in the Parisian suburbs and other French cities in late 2005], the producer was interviewed by all the media, French and foreign. It was the first time he had been asked his opinion, as an authority on the *banlieues*: eleven years earlier he had foretold what would happen, but of course, "it was just a film!"

AV Ezra Pound was right, I think, when he said artists were "the antennae of the race" (although I'd prefer "species"): they allow us to anticipate what is going to happen.

AJ To my mind, what happened with *La haine* shows three things. The first is that art can foretell, warn. The second is that it has no effect and nobody listens. And the third is that, even so, there is a ray of light: people can see that there are artists capable of sensing what is going on, and working with what they sense. And that they should be listened to.

A LIGHT IN THE DARKNESS

BC About the impossibility of separating ethics from aesthetics, you often quote Godard: "It may be true that one has to choose between ethics and aesthetics, but it is no less true that whichever one chooses, one will always find the other at the end of the road." We were discussing this a while ago, the way that, despite all that is said, you are an artist whose work makes a very powerful connection between art and life; and that this connection looks a bit awkward now, naïve even; it's seen as a dream, a rather unsuccessful avant-garde utopia... In fact, your strong interest in showing up the harsher aspects of the social praxis and basing interventions on them has often given rise to pejorative comments, things like you're the UNESCO artist or the UN artist. What do you think about that?

AJ It all comes down to a lack of information about my work. In a recent seminar on *Pictures of Atrocity*, [16] there was actually an argument with a UNESCO representative about their insulting and exploitative use of photography. Actually, I'd love to be the UNESCO artist, it would be a fantastic challenge: I would radically alter their use of photography, the way they portray children... Of course, I do a great variety of things. I have actually worked with organizations like that, for fund-raising. With Médecins sans Frontières, for example, and my strategy was very different from their usual one and gave extraordinary results. [17]

BC Something else that has a bearing on the same thing. A while ago, Jacques Rancière gave a conference in Chile in which he attacked a kind of pleasure today's art takes in catastrophe. He talked about an "ethical shift" in a very special sense, a kind of brutal skepticism in today's art that reduces it to just a never-ending archive of remnants, devoid of any urge for polemic that might help bring about emancipation. There's a lot of skepticism in your work, true, because the facts of catastrophe are so evident, but it's a skepticism that, in the face of everything, keeps raising that seminal question we spoke of earlier, the question about happiness. I think that, despite everything, that question is still an urgent force in your work, and it is precisely that which makes it political... I think you're still looking for reasons to trust in the human species, even if they're hard to find.

AJ There is always an element of light: I need it. It's true that it's in a very dark setting. I always wonder how much light I should let through: it's a key element in the program. It's something objective, an element of hope. It's there in every work. It's not so plain in some, but it's there. It's because of that light that I can carry on making them.

SA Does it have to do with seeing people in close-up? Beyond the face...

AV Or with human gestures? With the *punctum* of the gesture, totally recognizable, of children's arms, something like a *punctum* of common humanity, the only thing that is always recovered; the only thing that brings some light even in the worst situation?

Various That came out very Catholic. But we won't rub your nose in it, even though it did go on tape... (*laughter*)

RZ Within your work: I was thinking about how to outline a kind of visual grammar. Basically boxes of transparencies, ricochets, refractions... Some subphysical aspect of light. I feel that all your work has to do with light. That it bears light's seed of grammatical instability. I was thinking which of your works I liked best: I remember one which is just intersecting frames and body parts—it might be *Unframed*... I'm thinking about a kind of vocabulary of your work. In that work there were no faces and no scenes. While I agree with what's been said about the face and the scene, that work basically consisted of dislocated frames with body parts... It was a very physical work. It had a baroque purity.

AV A laconic purity. Laconicism is as baroque as you can get, don't you think?

A CELL—AND THE ART WORLD:
"WHO WE ADDRESS, WHAT CHANGES WE BRING ABOUT"

BC Why did you do this work on Gramsci?

AJ Because of what is happening in Italy today, which is nothing less than dramatic. I wanted to throw Gramsci in Berlusconi's face. It's specific to what is happening today. There is fascism in the air in the United States, Russia, and Italy, in my view. And I just couldn't exhibit in Italy without allowing myself that pleasure...

RZ Is the cell modeled on Gramsci's?

AJ Gramsci was physically very short. I made it very high so that the viewer would feel small... The Cell is about the role of culture today. A cell for the world of art... It's not meant as a historical reconstruction. Rather, it's about who we address, what changes we bring about. We've created a culture which is an infinite cell. I made that work to create this infinite, dramatic perspective... All of culture in a cell, it's a very negative, very pessimistic work. Sometimes I think, here you are talking to me, and I'm talking to you, and the result is zero.

AV There's Habermas's famous phrase: no revolutionary effect has derived from transgressions in the field of art... Xavier Rubert de Ventós wrote about *El arte ensimismado*—self-absorbed art. And now—I'm thinking of Ticio Escobar's *El arte fuera de sí*—there's an interest in an art that retains certain ritual functions, that does not insist on an autonomy which turns art into a prison.

AMR We're like people riding an exercise bike: puffing away, but getting nowhere.

AJ In *Let One Hundred Flowers Bloom*, the idea was to subject the flowers to two opposing forces, to make a rough metaphor for the situation of intellectuals in Italy today.

SA What was it like working with organic materials?

PC I like that... "organic"... like the "organic intellectual" Gramsci spoke of. The work cites prison, the tomb, the greenhouse, forms of confinement, it's all there.

RZ Of course. Certain activities, intellectual ones, kept in isolation, in special conditions...

AJ Speaking of the isolation of art, and the attempt to have a direct influence, I remember two works I brought up at the seminar on art education I did with Pablo Oyarzún. At the Venice Biennale, two artists proposed as a project that Fidel Castro should lease them the Guantanamo naval base—where we know acts of torture are taking place. It's a kind of non-place where the United States does what it wants. The United States pays Cuba 4,800 dollars a year to rent Guantanamo, under a treaty from many years ago. Fidel Castro keeps the checks, he doesn't cash them, because he wants the base back... The artists—who are Swiss and Italian—are going to go to the Supreme Court and assert that they are the new owners of the lease, and so the United States should vacate the base... Nothing will come of it, of course... [18]

AV But the media will cover it... Something will come of it in the field of information.

AJ It's a brilliant gesture. It's comparable with another work, by Beuys: his proposal to raise the Berlin Wall by five centimeters, to give it the "ideal proportions"... This was long before the Wall came down... [19]

BC Where does activism end and art begin in projects of this type? This question goes a bit against the grain of what I already know.

AJ I don't know where the dividing line is. To me there's no difference. It's whatever there's room for in the world of culture. Don't just think like an artist: think like a human being. The world of culture has a place where you can do it.

[1] The *copihue* is the Chilean bell flower, a national symbol.

[2] A reference to *Lights in the City*, Montreal, 1999, mounted in the dome of Bonsecours Market, which lit up whenever a homeless citizen entered a night shelter and pressed a button.

[3] A non-profit corporation that operates work safety programs and accident insurance.

[4] See Charles Harrison and Paul Wood (eds.), *Art in Theory 1900-2000*, London, Blackwell Publishers, 1992.

[5] This refers to an introduction in which Buchloh says that he did not complete any essays about women artists until 1982 because he was possibly following "if totally unconsciously, the rules of patriarchal order and the correlative psychological investment that often governs conventional artist-critic and artist-curator relationships." (Benjamin Buchloh, *Neo-Avantgarde and Culture Industry, Essays on European and American Art from 1955 to 1975,* Cambridge, Massachusetts/London, An October Book, The MIT Press, 2000, p.XXVIII). The reference to his women companions (see below) can be found in the acknowledgements, pp.XIV and XV.

[6] David Lamelas (Buenos Aires, 1946) currently lives and works between Paris, Berlin, and Los Angeles. Over the last three decades his work has included installations, photography and films, such as *L.A. Friends*, *Time as Activity* and *People and Time*.

[7] La batalla de Chile is a three-part documentary on the 1973 *coup d'état* and the events leading up to it, directed by Patricio Guzmán in the 1970s. In *La memoria obstinada* (1997), Guzmán reviewed the events with some of those who participated in these earlier documentaries.

[8] The group exhibition "In/Out: Four Projects by Chilean Artists" was held at the Washington Project for the Arts, Washington, D.C., in 1983.

[9] Nelly Richard, "Margins and Institutions (Art in Chile since 1973)," published in article form in *Art and Text*, no. 21, special issue, Melbourne, May-July 1986.

[10] Peter Osborne, *Conceptual Art*, London, Phaidon, 2002.

[11] Adriana Valdés.

[12] *Signs of Life* (1994).

[13] A reference to the arguments made in *Empire* by Michael Hardt and Antonio Negri, Cambridge, Massachusetts, Harvard University Press, 2001.

[14] Small boats often used for clandestine immigration.

[15] Produced by Mathieu Kassovitz and released in France in 1995.

[16] City University of New York, CUNY, December 2005.

[17] A reference to *The Gift*, Stockholm, 1998.

[18] "Guantanamo Initiative" is a work by Christoph Büchel and Gianni Motti, and it was presented at the Venice Biennale in 2004.

[19] In 1964.

JAAR
SCL
2006

Works in the exhibition

A logo for America 1987

Out of Balance 1989

Untitled (Water) 1990

The Silence of Nduwayezu 1997

Lament of the Images 2002

Searching for Gramsci 2004

Infinite Cell 2004

Let One Hundred Flowers Bloom 2005

Muxima 2005

A Logo for America 1987

CAMERAS
COPIERS
VIDEO

MINOLTA

THIS IS
NOT
AMERICA

The site and the formula

Rodrigo Zúñiga C.

Anyone reviewing Alfredo Jaar's artistic output by browsing through the pages of his catalogs and compilations will easily see many major milestones, equally outstanding, in the corpus of his work. While fully acknowledging the risk involved in investing one or other of these milestones with some kind of "inaugural" status in relation to the others, however, it may be possible to say that there have been moments in time, happy combinations of circumstances, that have strongly marked the development of this superb artist's work.

Moments in time, I say—with some hesitation. What is really operating here is the fruitful union between creative maturity and the artist's own demands upon himself, together with an unhesitating willingness to take risks. But I do not think it would be excessive to dwell on the implications and meaning of one year in particular, 1987. It was in that period, when the artist was just over thirty, that one of the most intense and fruitful turning points in his work occurred. As evidence of this, it may be enough to mention Jaar's participation in two events of recognized international prestige: the São Paulo Biennial (with his installation *Learning to Play*) and the eighth version of Documenta, in the German city of Kassel. Jaar participated in Documenta with one of his most accomplished works, and one that I consider particularly resonant in the establishment of a specific objectual, thematic and political grammar within his output: *1+1+1*. Along with these two interventions, which were evidence of the increasing notice being taken of this artist around the world (Alfredo Jaar was the first Latin American artist to be invited to exhibit in Documenta, at that time an exclusive enclave of first-world cultural hegemony), we need to consider another crucial piece, which operated in a different territory from the two works just mentioned. This intervention, entitled *A Logo for America*, had as its setting the imposing crossroads of Times Square in New York.

It will soon be twenty years since this public intervention was fleetingly (but calculatedly) activated on the Spectacolor sign, which competes with the other luminous displays crowding Times Square. Twenty years in which it has circulated in innumerable books and Internet photographs, and in the form of animations and revisions that can be found on the artist's own web site. And, above all, twenty years of respectful mention in many cultural forums, and in different reckonings of the most significant "political art" of the twentieth century. Over this period, *A Logo for America* has become an image that any one of us can easily recognize, as though through the workings of an odd preconscious sympathy. Perhaps it is in the force with which it articulates its message, in that visual power which permeates to the very dimensions of something we seem already to have glimpsed and recalled, that the exemplary quality of this work of Alfredo Jaar's resides.

From 1987, with its electronic staging in Times Square, to 2006, with its documentary reinstallation in the artist's exhibition in Santiago, Chile, this work has traveled a long road, but without ever losing that original feeling of *impertinence*. The vigor and skillfulness of Jaar' strategy can resonate, still, as a stirring of perplexity and questioning. It is the purpose of what now follows to try to make out some clues in this direction.

A reserve of light

In that year, 1987, Alfredo Jaar was offered a unique opportunity to give concrete expression, out in the open (in the middle of a bustling and overwhelmingly cosmopolitan city), to some of the strategic and political considerations foreshadowed in many of his earlier works. As part of a group of thirty or so artists chosen by Public Art Fund in New York (an institution that had already sponsored artists like Jenny Holzer, in 1982, and Barbara Kruger, in 1983, on the same terms), he obtained access to a computerized light screen whose prominent position and visibility created intriguing staging possibilities in that urban landscape.

The opportunity to position oneself, for forty-five seconds every six minutes over a month, in the noisy epicenter of New York's arteries is fraught with potential, of course, but also with risk. At the very least, the advertising format of the work brings with it something very like an immolation: to project upon that landscape a "message" or an "image" that permits itself some kind of *artistic* attribute as a condition for its acceptance assumes a tacit receptiveness which naturally becomes extremely fragile in the incombustible roar of the metropolis. Because the scene created would be intermittent, again, and would be crowded in upon by the procession of other advertising images, the challenge was compounded by the need to work with two factors that were difficult to process in this case: effectiveness, and the overwhelming nature of the site.

The artist, then, had to "make light" in an unfruitful, clamorous situation overloaded with strident advertising, overwhelmed by relentless visual manipulation and disharmony. But Jaar's works, even then, already "knew" something about light. And more than that: as rarely happens with contemporary artists, Alfredo Jaar began very early on to create a fine mesh of "stereoscopic" relationships around the sites of his interventions. His works made use of lightboxes, fissured frames and surrounds, mirrors, ricochets of light on crystal-line or opaque surfaces, reverberations, positional breaks (take *Rushes* or *Welcome to the Third World*, from 1986, or *Frame of Mind, 1+1+1* or *Persona*, from 1987). This would intensify over the coming years and, around the mid-1990s, would give rise to an intensive reflection on photographic reproduction as an artistic resource and on the politics of representation. By that time, though, his "scenic" vocabulary had already produced an abundance of striking examples of a *sui generis* objectual and spatial construction. In the cases mentioned, Jaar's work gave clear examples of a highly revi-talizing and original conjunction of his sociocultural concerns with eminently baroque resources or strategies, threaded together by a visual language that drew upon divided imag-es, staging effects of varying intensity, blocked or fractured lights, unbalanced angles.

In particular, it could be said that Alfredo Jaar, trained in architecture and film, was already, to a large degree, an artist of the *Gestalt*, of spatial rhythms and intervals, of locations and fissures, of scansions. For this reason, the material vo-cation of his artistic operations demanded a rigorous, finely judged use of the light variable: its sources, its positioning in the different corners of a room, its careful dispensation, its intersection and mingling with the other elements of the *mise en scène*. The artist's frequent use of the Cibachrome format, which might now be said to be a hallmark of his work, may perhaps be the best possible condensation of the intrin-sically luminescent quality of these operations. Jaar's work is unashamedly physical; notwithstanding its bold discur-siveness, it has succeeded in remaining true to a somatic, *aesthetic* quality which began to emerge at this almost non-material, infraphysical level of the reflection, the wake, the dispersed light. The mesh of light is the perennial infrastructure in the materiality of Jaar's work.

While in many of the artist's installations the staging is dynamic and evanescent, constituted by blocked or released particles or streams of light, it is no less true that on innumerable occasions light has become embodied, been formed into letters: writing. A light that is sometimes armored in a neon casing, for example, and that confined in this or some other way is deposited on walls, on water, on public buildings, on churches. Traced on these surfaces, it marks them with names of cities, individuals, quotations from poems. Even when Jaar has used typography to write names on other surfaces (names of survivors or of films, phrases or thoughts), it is striking that this resource has worked as though by echoing a light *in absentia*—as though the mention of the name ignited a presence, or brought the absent one, the murmuring shadow of that name, into the light.

So it is, then, that Jaar's visual interventions have been dedicated to a solemn rewriting of the *scenic space* appropriated for the artistic operation, as a way of remaking the defiled tissue of the body of the image in the "society of the spectacle," and of compelling a long overdue visual reflection in the era of programmed media blindness. Before anything else, though, this shrewd and far-sighted aspiration is materialized as a *reserve of light*. Because of this, and because of all that relates to light and the whole sequel of possible allegories which follow on from it (invisibility, transparency, unstageable presence, the impossibility of presentation), one cannot simply force one's way into Jaar's work by wielding references, implicit or otherwise, to the biblical account of Genesis (Let there be light...), or the centuries-old traditions of iconoclasm, or the analysis of the sublime in our own times.

Rather, Jaar's staging devices have very ingeniously refined the material and technological resources and textures of light. In the space surrounding the viewer, he conjoins the rhetorical and articulative possibilities of light with the challenge that is present in every one of this artist's works: how to *make light* and reclaim the power of the image *in* the artwork to move us affectively. "What are artists for in times of barbarism?" seems to be Jaar's question, rather in Hölderlin's elegiac tone. "How can one live up to the *promise* of art, and of what it may still be capable of safeguarding? How can one extend that promise in the present day?" In Jaar's eyes, only art seems capable of appealing to the affective mode of an individual in such a way as to mobilize, in silence, the virtual constitution of a kind of *e-motive community*—a community in movement, in intense dialogue, affectively, politically and culturally engaged. From this perspective, Jaar's artistic labor seeks to *shed light* on the very core of co-habitation, of being-in-common.

A corollary of the above: *A Logo for America*, the work we are concerned with here, was demarcated by the increasing imperiousness of this drive, of these problems; by this imperative which sought to link the scenic materialization of luminescence with the *poietic*, luminous, fructifying need for personal and collective engagement. In which to pronounce the word "luminous" is to enter into the very heart of the perplexity. To make light: to open up a crack, precipitate a crisis, provide matter for thought. Making light, in this case, in the petrified mechanism of signification, of cultural representation that is usurped and naturalized. Making light for "communities that lack images," in the artist's words—that is, images "cut loose" from the community realm. *This is Not America*, that is how the computerized animation will begin on to the imposing structures of Times Square.

Animation and calligram

With an intervention like *A Logo for America*, Jaar's diffident scenic calm seems to have been reconfigured as protest, as provocation. Light no longer carries a specific quantum of calculation depending on the location; it is poured out, rather, like blazing publicity, as though it were mingling, surreptitiously, into the bloodstream of the system of image circulation.

What, then, might be the *visibility* effect with which this work is operating? What is it *casting light* upon? And what type of light, now that it is making use of a visual resource which is entangled with the tumult of a mega-city? What might it mean, in these circumstances, to *move* the viewer, co-habit suddenly, in the space of just a few seconds, with the viewer's own movement through these very streets?

The animation produced by Alfredo Jaar, as those who have visited this exhibition will know for themselves, lasts just a few seconds. In that short space, the artist offers a remarkable visual choreography: geometrical shapes and statements that slide over the screen, turning, emerging and disappearing, in the way of advertisements when they celebrate the projected virtues of their products. In this case, Jaar constructs his visual narrative around the word "America." Around the word, yes; but the first thing to come in sight in this animation is a drawing that is unequivocally of the country—not the continent—which has peremptorily arrogated to itself the ownership of the name "America," the United States. Then the drawing becomes a calligram: from this same outline of the map of the United States a direct, simple, and ringing phrase emerges and explodes into forthright accusation: "This is not America." The first friction between image and name, between "objective" representation and exultant self-denomination. The second friction: the United States flag, first in color, and then emptied of it, and the verdict: "This is not America's flag." Michel Foucault said that the calligram secretly reinstated a former unity between image and name by creating a taut intersection and confluence between the arrangement of the verbal statement and the realm of the figure;[1] in this case, it is the actual figure (the map, the flag) that is imposed first of all in order to refute or de-authorize what the conjunction of its calligram implies: that this map, or this flag, is, represents, "America."

This being so, the calligrammatic disjunction in Jaar's animated sequence acts as a minor cataclysm in the representation. Immediately—to return to the "narrative" of the animation—the word "America," until then the subject of two powerful refutations, emerges on its own. The narrative drive then focuses especially on the letter R, from which a semicircle and a triangle are formed. Bit by bit, these forms shift and swivel until they erupt into the recognizable profile of the whole American continent, north to south. This unfolding outline obliterates the word "America" across the whole width of the screen; its contours then re-form bit by bit until, in a kind of exuberant climax to the encounter between name and figure (now the whole continent), they restore the word "America," but this time replacing the letter R with the "legitimate" outline of the American continent. It is this last image that is finally left in possession of the screen.

In this work, everything would seem to have come together in a happy consecration of "site and formula," to use Rimbaud's expression. The site, Times Square; the formula, a brief narrative, not without its subtle innocence, in which the protagonists are a word, some geometric shapes, and a few phrases, and their disturbing convulsions on that screen of light. Its air of innocence notwithstanding, it is almost needless to recall the wave of astonishment and disbelief it was able to arouse among the United States public.

Perhaps one of the most striking features of this public intervention is the way it succeeded, during the few moments it flashed up, in activating an apparently minor linguistic disagreement that nonetheless goes to the root of a far-reaching ideological conflict, with a variety of implications for the forms by which the common existence of the continent's peoples is regulated. This whole conflict is evoked by the mere mention—the sole, automatic attribution—of the word "America." The phrase "This is not America" seems a diffident response to the intimidating and dishearteningly routine conviction (often fomented even by ourselves) that they, the "Americans" of the United States, the "real" Americans, will not let us "be American." A "mere" word, you might think; but a word which immediately forces you to position yourself on one side or other of the dividing line, and which instantly introduces a dichotomy between "them" and "us." "They," sure enough, sensed that this intervention meant an attack on the symbolic order, and reacted; for us, on the other hand, it is obvious that "this" is not "America's" flag.

Simply yet effectively, this emblem, this standard constructed by the phrase "This is not America" decodes the powerful imposition wrought by the calligram mentioned earlier: the calligram that, quite casually and spontaneously, conjoins the map of the United States, the United States flag, and the word "America." A calligram that is its own legitimation, that enjoys the tautological privilege of naming itself and representing itself. In this succinct exercise of Jaar's, there hovers the shadow—always ephemeral, always unperceived —of the political production of meaning, the violence latent in the structure of signification. By turning the manipulation of language and the political forms of representation back upon themselves, the proposal to create "a *logo* for the American continent" hints at the way a single word can cover a whole substratum of hegemonic relationships; the way the "common currency" of names and their authorized attributions operates as part of the invisible, interconnective traffic of the formations of power.

In the work being discussed here, there are no viewfinders or special optical devices; there are no frames, or mirrors, or scenic discontinuities. Only lights pulsing from the top of a building, like the advertisements that roll smoothly past on all sides. Amid the neon intrusion of dazzling, hypnotic proclamations forced upon the attention of passers-by, amid the numbing washes of light broken down by the phosphorescence of advertising into their constituent bursts, this incisive artistic operation stands out like a barely protruding cuticle, a tiny irregularity. In the middle of the no-man's-land of light that is Times Square, one fine strand of rhythm runs strangely counter to the glowing pulse of the avenue.

For clearly, however paradoxical it may seem, Jaar's stratagem worked by *subtraction*. The established light was subtracted from by *another* light. It illuminated, brought to light, the collision latent in the order of names. A single name, in this case: "America." It precipitated language into a referential crisis, and the explosive effect of this was to tear away the customary, stereotypical, political thinking that had given names their protective layer. This intervention of light provided the exact measure of the political materiality of language. And we are all aware of what fatal consequences arise when anyone claims to speak on behalf of language.

In *A Logo for America*, therefore, language, the invisible support of our structure of meaning, was shown up as a delicate layer, any interference with which immediately produces an effect of precipitation and violence, however little Jaar's visual procedure may intend any violent act. To scratch language and its orders of representation is like opening skin to the air: a diffuse work with the intractable materiality of the non-material. It is odd to think what manner of bite could open skin to the air, what kind of scratch—swift and light, almost too fast to see—might gash the transparency we breathe. Air, light or language, in this work Alfredo Jaar knew how to inflict that wound.

[1] Cf. Michel Foucault, *This is Not a Pipe*, Berkeley, University of California Press, 1983, trans. James Harkness.

Untitled (Water) 1990

Out of Balance 1989

The Liquid Drift of the Eye
Ana María Risco

Imagine you could peel away the clean, orderly arrangements of plane and texture that Alfredo Jaar's installations usually present: perhaps what you would gradually reveal, underlying this formal precision and control, is an eye striving intrepidly to break loose, to free itself. This eye knows that its cultural frameworks and the constraints it operates under derive only tangentially from the analytical tradition of art; it does perceive, though, a radical threat to its freedom from the politico-economic machinery by which the great image of the spectacle is produced.

The works referred to in this text—*Untitled (water)* and *Out of Balance*—were produced between the late 1980s and the early 1990s. They illustrate, I think, with singular clarity how the striving for optical emancipation which has seemed to be at work within Jaar's politico-visual project for more than fifteen years underlies, almost like an instinctive force, the finely wrought and lucid apparatus of perception that this project has gradually shaped.

The fusing of two needs can be sensed in the calculated elaboration of these two installations. The first is the artist's need to expand and develop—setting out from his own travels and first-hand research—the critical sensibilities required to discover and "realize" the image that is obstructed by communications and made elusive to the eye. The second, arising in the actual labor of composition, is the need to find a formula of presentation that will allow him to save the image thus obtained from the impotence and emptiness which mere circulation would almost certainly entail.

Conceived at a time of intense experimentation, what these two works are attempting, in the specificity of their purpose and operations, is to keep their images from being apprehended so rapidly that they are thereby neutralized. By deliberately slowing the speed at which these can be perused—by means of resources such as sections and breaks, lighting effects, reflections, imbalances in composition or the occupation of negative spaces of communication—they seek to reimpose the waiting times that must necessarily elapse between the conditioned, automatic act of looking and the possibility—informed by experience, and always delayed—of seeing.

These installations rely for their analytical drift on mobility and the dislocation of visual habits, thanks to the studied arrangement of their components in space. They subject viewers to a form of displacement, flexing, curvature, that takes them out of their accustomed cultural orbits and, once outside this solid framework, guides them toward other waters.

Open waters

Advertising imagery, wholly visible yet blinding to the viewer, is a material whose powerful conditionings Alfredo Jaar often uses to good effect. For anyone coming face to face with the installation *Untitled (water)*, the imagery used in tourist advertising to administer the photographic representation of the sea will probably loom large for a moment, before being swallowed up in the optical space conditioned by the work. Required to become an object of desire, to nurse the elemental fantasy of holiday freedom and relaxation, this seductive and much-used image of an expanse of seawater furrowed by a cruise ship, whose presence is indicated by its foaming wake, shimmers for a second—only to be dismantled. On this same intense blue, on this same extravagant promise, *Untitled (water)* is projecting another journey, addressing another contingency of travel, but this time on the mental reverse of the advertising image.

On the rear of the lightboxes that the viewer encounters upon entering the room, there are pictures of travelers who are not tourists. Different shots of men, women and children whose South Asian features are fragmented by a wire fence. Immigrants, like so many of those who cross the world's borders. They are Vietnamese—as we learn from the information accompanying the work—who have crossed stretches of open sea in an attempt to reach and settle on the promising economic soil of Hong Kong. They have fled poverty, hunger and lack of opportunity; in so doing, they have brought themselves within reach of prison. Discouraged or expectant, they wait in their confinement for a court to grant or deny them refugee status.[1] Yet in these pictures, taken by Jaar just before the end of his fact-finding visit to these prisons, they are almost smiling. They say their farewells to someone who has been able to leave freely, bearing, as a traveler, a record that he will reinstall at the other end of the earth. A spectator who does not look upon them with an explorer's curiosity, who will bear their image not as exotic merchandise from the Orient, but as testimony to a historical and political problem of global dimensions.

After the first contact with the installation, but before fully entering it, there is a moment of suspense. As you are drawn in by the sparkling water and prepare to approach the six lightboxes, which are separated by narrow gaps, a first reading suggests itself. Thirty mirrors lining the rear wall reflect back fragments of your own image, corners of the room you are standing in, small pieces of your certainty. Unexpectedly, as you move about, these familiar images are joined by glimpses of those "others," hidden or kept back, as they have been till then, on the back of the lightboxes. Distant, unknown others who slowly reveal themselves as dispossessed and imprisoned Asians with each expectant step. The unsettling exploration continues. To choose a viewpoint is to opt for a narrative. To see them and yourself in a shifting dynamic. To select and combine fragments for a provisional syntax. Three journeys—yours, the immigrants' and the artist's—thus come into contact. There is no form of words to sanction the encounter, and the image of the sea now has a feeling of adventurousness about it. Just where advertising would drive home its appeal with a phrase (like the ironic "opening new doors" which Jaar projected in another of his works on the Asian prisons), all that is allowed to flow in *Untitled (water)* is the probability of an initial contact.

Historical frontiers

In this work, as in others whose documentary images are taken from the United States-Mexico border or the stretch of the Atlantic crossed by Haitians on their way to Florida, Jaar has chosen to enter a vital and treacherous zone of the narrative of modernity.

Right from the outset, immigration played a silent but active part in the history of the modern nation. As Eric Hobsbawm has observed, immigrants' status as exiles and second-class citizens was caused not only by the segregationist outlook of dominant groups, but also by those who took upon themselves the territorial defense of proletarian labor conditions,[2] and they gave this outlook a slogan and an ideological basis. The territorial and cultural boundaries defended by the great powers during the "age of empire" (strategically open to the movement of colonizers, goods and slaves) contrasted then with other frontiers, weak and insignificant, that were unable to check the advance of colonization.

Now, when a vast economic network is being brought into being and the nation-state model that organized the last two centuries is entering into crisis, boundaries are being evaluated by new standards. They are more permeable and open to trade in goods and capital, while increasingly "intelligent" (technologically speaking) reinforced prisons and walls are being put up to prevent the passage of people. Movement, travel, threatens labor markets and creates uncertainty in privileged, settled populations. Nonetheless, those who do not benefit from that stability (because it means war or hunger) travel anyway. Mass immigration still traces a broad line from East to West and from former colonies to former colonizers, but these movements are following ever more circumscribed routes, from poor countries to less poor ones or to areas that offer only a minimum of peace and employment. [3] Through danger and exile these defectors seek what a globalized economy cannot give them, and for Hardt and Negri they form a massive and growing picture of a nomadic "counter-empire." [4]

Untitled (water) is not designed to address the political situation of displaced persons by means of words. What it does, rather, is to set the stage for people to experience exile and movement in their own person. No sequence of arguments, no ordering of its components; instead, the experience is embodied in the person who must physically move to read it. Rather than giving priority to one standpoint from which the story of the Vietnamese prisoners can be grasped in its entirety, the installation instead demands an effort of perception mediated by the splintering of the image which the gaps and mirrors produce, its *reflection* generating a syntax between the viewer's own image—which organizes identity —and that of these "others." A liberating gymnastics, like that which an acute observer, Frantz Fanon, observed in the tribal dancing of colonized Africans, [5] seems to be demanded as a viewing strategy. An exorcizing mobility that releases us as viewers from the constraints of normal visuality, the conditionings of the circulating image, and the cryptic frameworks of art, and enables us to feel our way to an encounter with the uncertainty, and thus the experience, of these "others."

The fluid in-between

The method thus used by Jaar to give visibility to the situation of the displaced is the realization of the twofold strategy touched upon at the beginning of this text. On the one hand, the works dealing with this situation—not just *Untitled (water)*, but also others such as *Coyote* (1988), *Fading* (1989-91-93), *Je me souviens* (1992), *Walking on Water* (1992),

Bonjour Sécurité (1993), *Crossing* (1993)—create the conditions for a closer approach to the rigors of the migratory journey, exacerbated by hazardous conditions, political barriers and xenophobia; on the other, they grapple with modes of seeing and representation that come from the logic of frontiers and segregation on which this experience depends. The work does not become detached from the contingency of the displaced, which Jaar always deals with in the particular, to the extent of treating as a medium the actual image of these people, their vital needs, their outraged struggles and their hard journeys. However, the work is also, formally, a discourse on abstract frontiers: demarcation points that link up the space of representation, creating protectionist barriers and marking out territories that are off limits to movements of the eye or thought.

It is not by chance that liquid is so prominently featured in these works of Jaar's on the displaced. While the image of the sea refers in the first instance to water as a dangerous medium (an ambiguous one since it is also an obstacle) often used to elude frontier controls, its potential for evoking uncertainty and mobility, promise or threat, is also an invitation to reconsider the set parameters wherein the very act of looking is organized.

This is reinforced by the complex web of relationships involved in migration. What comes into play here is not only a policy regulated, as far as possible, by international organizations, but particular and subtle cultural processes for which there is no provision in border logics or bilateral diplomatic agreements. The situation of displaced communities often reproduces, in the territory of their enclave, the ideological frameworks of the old colonialism, with its well-known fantasies about the volume and direction of cultural flows between the communities brought into contact. In these encounters, the way people regard one another is crucial and creates boundaries more potent than physical frontiers.

The image of the seas—foaming, dangerous, uncontrollable, unending—that have historically joined and divided peoples and provided the opportunity for journeys, discoveries, violent invasions and also happier encounters, ties in with that *in-between* where, as Homi Bhabha perceives it,[6] an unpredictable cultural space is generated, one that does not really bear the imprint of either tradition, that cannot be controlled from either side, but that belongs to the in-between place where the symbolic fields dominating the one and the other are liquefied, dissolved and intermingled. In this liquid territory the identities of the different cultural groups make a genuine appearance, and they too are composed of fluid, shifting subjectivities that are hard to pin down, never the same as their own selves or their supposed definition, but mutually referential in their burgeoning construction. In this in-between place, where each identity hosts and produces its other, at this "Rimbaudian edge,"[7] as Adriana Valdés has called it, there is an opening for new thinking about immigrants as a rising historical presence and as a political blueprint for the design of a new mental geography.

Faltering in the image

If fragmentation and the in-between are critical dimensions in *Untitled (water)*, visual imbalance, the discursive power of the frame and the elimination of context take on analytical importance in *Out of Balance*, a work that Jaar presented a year earlier, in 1989.

In the three-walled room where it is being exhibited in Santiago, no image is at eye level. Above or below the eye line, there are long white rectangles—the lightbox as outline—with faces pressed up close to their edges. Marginalized within the rectangle and unbalanced in space, these faces speak by default. Twice denied, they yet have a message of affirmation. If you step back to see the higher images, or bend to look at the lower part of the wall, you can engage with those feverish eyes, with those muddy faces that tell nothing and reveal everything from their precarious position.

Overdetermined by the careful apportionment of spaces, by the odd shapes that intersect it, by the small patches of figuration and the long expanses of white that dominate it, the room shines like an inscriptive surface. It is experienced, too, like a stripped-down publication project, deliberately displaying the lines, noises, silences and omissions with which it skews the vision it elaborates and projects. The pictures and those portrayed in them raise questions enough as it is, but their import is modulated by the way this apparition has been handled. Who are these men looking out from the white corner? What weight that we cannot see has dragged them over to the edge of the picture?

Golden composition

It was in about 1985 that Jaar began to process the story so tersely recounted by these faces. The research began with a journey (the first of many he was to make later to other places and with other projects) to Serra Pelada in the Brazilian Amazon. After a lengthy, careful approach, he began to photograph the working routine of the gold prospectors, who had settled there in their hundreds of thousands since the late 1970s, when a huge gold deposit was discovered in the area. Although the zone was controlled by a powerful metals company, at that time state-owned and now in private hands, his visual investigation explored the work of the *garimpeiros*, who drilled into the hillside by hand or with home-made contrivances, seeking out nuggets of a metal that was of great importance for the dynamic of speculation in Brazil and around the world. He was probably greatly struck even then, in that field research, by how *unbalanced* the situation was: the muddy ground, the crude mining conditions, in such contrast to the glitter of the gold and the rich profits awaiting those who traded in it.

With his 1986 exhibition *Gold in the Morning*, held at a promi-
nent venue on the art circuit, the Venice Biennale, and with
Rushes, shown that same year in a very public place, the
Spring subway station in New York, these pictures of the
Serra Pelada miners became widely known and with them
Jaar's work, which obtained public recognition. Whereas
Gold in the Morning was already using negative spatializa-
tion as the critical core of its narrative, Rushes highlighted
the contrast between the imposing presence of the workers'
bodies and the volatility of the gold price, whose movements
were shown next to the workers' photographs. Perhaps only
market operators, seeing the exhibition on their way to Wall
Street, could *speculate* on its meaning, while most people
tried to place it in a recognizable context by reading it as
an enigmatic form of advertising.
Compared to these first two installations and to others that
subsequently drew on the documentary material from Serra
Pelada, such as *Frame of Mind* (1987) or *Unframed* (1992),
Out of Balance gives even less information about the miners,
entirely removing the details representing their environment.
As a result, the focus is now on the editorial decisions that
make them visible or invisible, on the relationship between
centrality and displacement, between those who dominate
and those who disappear in the dynamics of representation
as industry and spectacle, with proletarian faces and bodies
being paraded only occasionally at the margins. The frame
is central here as a tool of focus, composition and balance,
categories characteristic not only of the selective, combi-
natorial economy that makes any discourse possible, but of
much more: a political economy conditioned by strategies
that deliberately choose what should be made visible, what
passed over in silence.
If the fluidity of the works on displacements and the displaced creates opportunities to dissolve frontiers or make
them partially porous, at least in our minds, the frame which

dominates *Out of Balance* allows us to grasp the violent aspect of the shapes used to design and fragment the blank page of reality.

Fleeing the composition

Subjugating the unknown *other* by imposing frames, molds, prefigured images that reduce the need for communication, is a tried and tested formula for managing transcultural experiences, particularly those entailing subordination, now or in the past. One example will do: the wide spectrum of aberrant assumptions about America—its flora, fauna and population —on which the epistemological approach to the new world [8] was based and which has since been modified and updated to produce other patterns that are now used, in variously savage, surrealistic, marvelous and frightful forms, to organize the image projected on to Latin America from outside.

However, "fixity," as Homi Bhabha has perceived it from an eyewitness's standpoint, the attribution of prior identities and their reproduction in the syntax of segregationist discourses, is a paradoxical mode of representation. [9] It looms over the subordinated or marginal others (in this case, the Brazilian miners who form a large community of unsettled and displaced adventurers) in the suspicion that something is bound to come out from the margins, the exception or flight that rebuts determination. And indeed, it is perhaps by escaping from a preappointed place, dismantling the fence or, as Adriana Valdés puts it, avoiding the "Medusan stare" [10] which petrifies the other upon whom it falls, that the wandering and the marginalized can spontaneously exercise a critical power.

Deliberately shorn of their context, of the exotic connotations usually associated with the brutal labor of what is known as the third world, the miners' faces in this composition rebel against the trap or captivity of the frame. The unbalancing of their presentation can be read too, from another angle, as a sudden displacement whereby a visualized identity breaks out from the parameters of composition used to postulate it from outside. What is petrified by the Medusan stare in *Out of Balance* is the white part of the image, because the target of that stare has fled suddenly and subversively to the edge of the composition.

The frontiers of art

The relationship of Jaar's work with frontiers, with mobility in physical and mental spaces, expresses a special approach to geography and the political problems associated with its representation, analogous to the approach to the actual representation associated with the publication policies of geographical space.

A thought-provoking way of ending this essay on two works that look at reality from a displaced, dislocated, decentralized standpoint, or that deal with others who have been petrified and confined within territorial and mental limits, is to think how they challenge or call into question the very territory of art as a field with the status of relative autonomy so well described by Pierre Bourdieu, that is, as a self-regulating set of relationships between agents and institutions that possess the capital needed to occupy positions of dominance. [11]

The two works have been described and commented on jointly here to make their thematic kinship more evident to the viewer. They were intended by their author to be mounted in an exhibition space, to be seen within a context governed by the artistic field. It is, to all appearances, a privileged context which brings images under a kind of critical mantle; but like everywhere else, it is also permeated by dynamics of power, by a structure, indeed, that turns everything it touches into a commodity. Works like *Untitled (water)* or *Out of Balance*, or the others in this exhibition, acknowledge the codes which apply in that context and which could probably neutralize what they set out to do, by absorbing their strategy. As though shielding themselves from that situation, they are not fully explainable by these codes.

Jaar's work is, at the same time, something that takes place in the public space, in the form of interventions which are another crucial part of his activity, and that dislocates geographical space by setting forth a political outlook which, although site-specific, relates to contemporary problems and circumstances the world over. Not only does it set out to move freely across the frontier separating the artistic realm from the social one, but it looks out from art to what lies "outside" it, trying to produce and make visible, from this vantage point, a possible representation of what that "outside" prefers to keep in the shadows. If this is an image of horror, the work seems to say, it is better to see this than to see nothing.

The epigraph in the most recent publication on Alfredo Jaar's public interventions (*The Fire This Time*)[12] is a quote from James Baldwin that goes straight to the heart of the perspective with which I now end this text: "Life is more important than art, that's what makes art important."

In the first half of the twentieth century, Walter Benjamin established a tension that would subsequently describe a very radical oscillation between the aestheticization of politics and the politicization of art. [13] Now, at a time when other fires are burning, Alfredo Jaar's work would seem to be formulating a new practical variant on the unsolvable Benjaminian opposition: everything is political, and aesthetics, although it has tended to be viewed as a "field" with the drift of history, has no possible territory other than life itself.

¹ In 1988, the British administration of Hong Kong decided to place all Vietnamese asylum seekers reaching the island in detention centers, where they were to await the court's decision. The measure was clearly a dissuasion strategy to check the massive demand for asylum. During the 1990s, the newly established Chinese administration in Hong Kong eased the detention system to the point where it virtually disappeared, although it too arranged successive waves of repatriations with the Vietnamese government.

² See especially Eric Hobsbawm, *The Age of Empire, 1875-1914*, London, Vintage, 1989, chapter 6, "Waving Flags: Nations and Nationalism."

³ For a diagnosis of this new multidirectional aspect of contemporary immigration, see Stephen Castles and Mark J. Miller, *The Age of Migration. International Population Movements in the Modern World*, New York, The Guilford Press, 1993.

⁴ Michael Hardt and Antonio Negri, *Empire*, Cambridge, Massachusetts, Harvard University Press, 2001, chapter "Intermezzo: Counter-empire."

⁵ In *The Wretched of the Earth* (New York, Grove Press, 1965) Fanon notes how ritual dance operated as a safety valve for the members of colonized tribes in Africa who were subjected to strong cultural and physical pressures. "By various means," he writes, "—shakes of the head, bending of the spinal column, throwing of the whole body backward—may be deciphered as in an open book the huge effort of a community to exorcise itself, to liberate itself, to explain itself."

⁶ *In-between* is a wide-ranging concept which Homi Bhabha has used to arrive at alternative readings of the relationship between cultures, using parameters of reciprocal and horizontal contamination. The reference I am using is the article "Interrogating Identity" by Homi K. Bhabha, in *The Location of Culture*, London, Routledge, 1994.

⁷ Adriana Valdés, "Alfredo Jaar, imágenes entre culturas," in *Composición de lugar, escritos sobre cultura*, Santiago, Chile, Universitaria, 1996, p.97.

⁸ See Antonello Gerbi, *La disputa del nuevo mundo. Historia de una polémica, 1750-1900*, Mexico City, Fondo de Cultura Económica, 1982, second edition.

⁹ "The Other Question: Stereotype, Discrimination and the Discourse of Colonialism," in Homi Bhabha, *op. cit.*

¹⁰ Adriana Valdés, *op. cit.*, p.97.

¹¹ See Pierre Bourdieu, *Rules of Art: Genesis and Structure of the Literary Field*, Stanford, Stanford University Press, 1996, trans. Susan Emanuel.

¹² Nancy Princenthal and Mary Jane Jacob, *Alfredo Jaar: The Fire This Time. Public Interventions 1979-2005*, Milan, Charta, 2005.

¹³ Walter Benjamin, "The Work of Art in the Age of Mechanical Reproduction," in *Illuminations*, New York, Schocken, 1969, pp.217-252, trans. Harry Zohn.

The Silence of Nduwayezu 1997

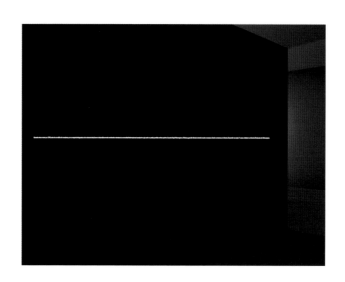

I will never forget his silence. The silence of Nduwayezu.

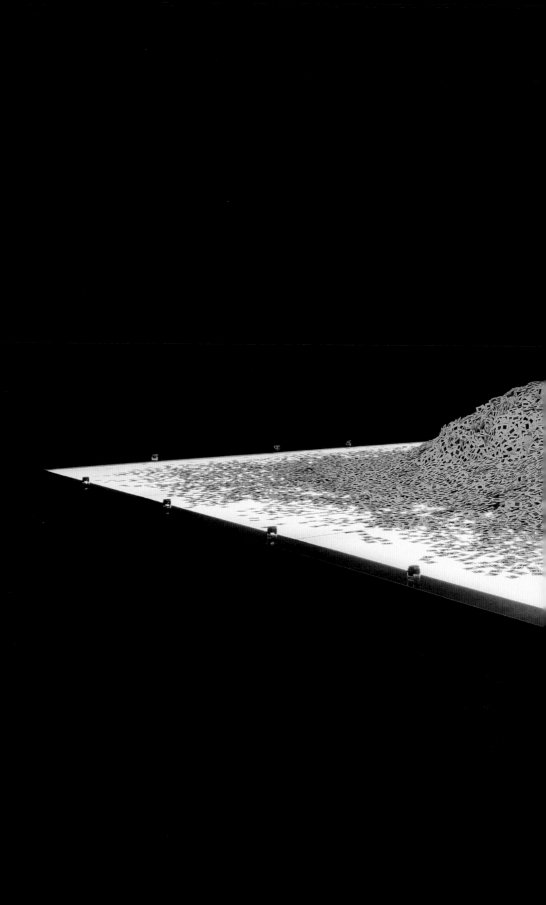

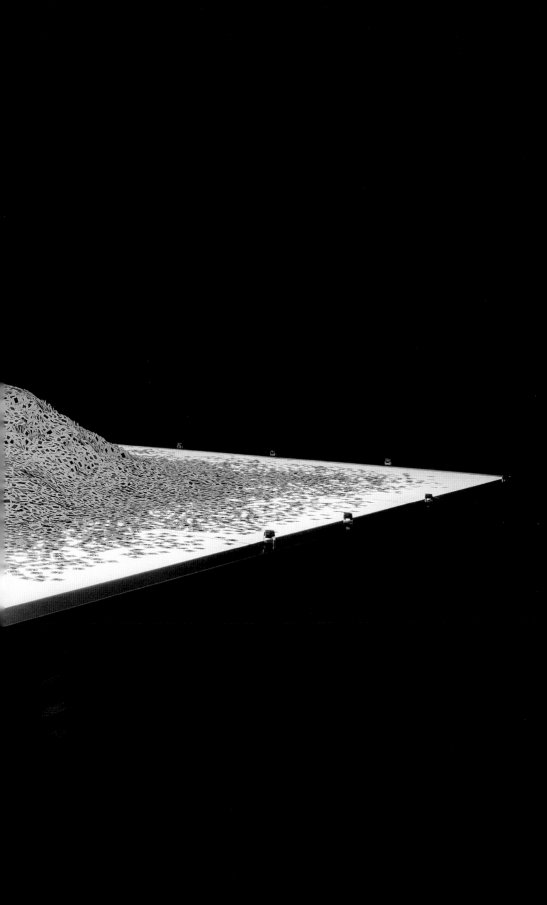

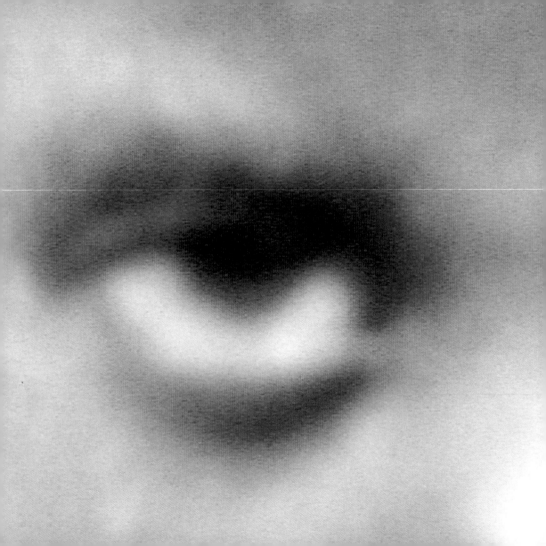

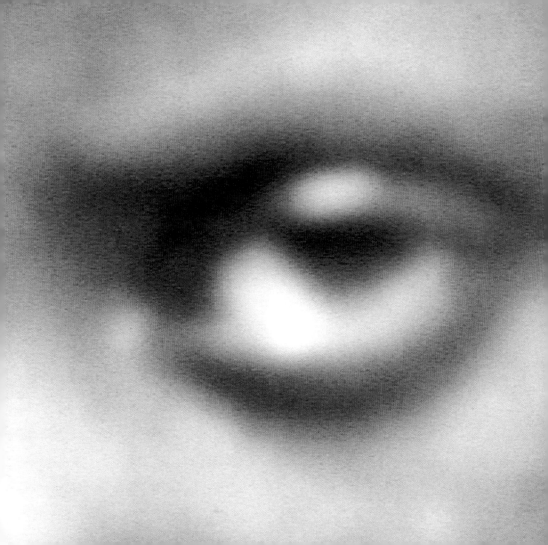

Practices of Devotion   Bruno Cuneo

"I am an invisible man [...] I am a man of substance, of flesh and bone, fiber and liquids—and I might even be said to possess a mind. I am invisible, understand, simply because people refuse to see me [...] That invisibility to which I refer occurs because of a peculiar disposition of the eyes of those with whom I come in contact."
Ralph Ellison, *Invisible Man*

"[...] Art has as its task to create in such a way that at all points of its surface the phenomenal, the appearance becomes an eye, the seat of the soul, rendering itself visible to the spirit."
W.G. Hegel

"Not only was I moved by that family of eyes, but I felt a little ashamed of our bottles and glasses, surpassing our thirst."
Charles Baudelaire, *Spleen de Paris*

Seeing without looking and, what is worse, without looking at others, is one of the most disturbing phenomena of our time. In public transport, waiting rooms, elevators, streets or stores, strong visual contact is virtually taboo (it is telling that so many people now choose to wear dark glasses), or is permitted only in that neutral, nervous, furtive, and purely utilitarian form that is sometimes termed "polite disinterest." In the symbolic order of our mass society, even this "deritualized regard"[1] must mean something: it is a sign, to begin with, of the oppressive fear people experience today (this was pointed out by Canetti, who termed it "blinding") of being touched by the unknown, and thereby losing possession of themselves or being wrenched out of their introversion by the relational intimacy that any genuine eye contact entails. The most remarkable allegory of this fear that I know of is

Samuel Beckett's *Film*, a short whose plot consists almost entirely in a headlong flight on foot by a terrified protagonist who refuses at every turn to look or be looked at, other than by a couple of inoffensive cats. Who knows, again, whether this stubborn refusal may not be the necessary outcome of an aberrant form of adaptive behavior whose function, in an environment where potentially destabilizing impressions or shocks abound, is to guarantee a degree of equilibrium in the mental economy of individuals, even if the price is an alarming increase in what we might call, with Simmel, *Blasiertheit*: jadedness.

Jadedness is not only the price but the common coin of our current social and visual system. For the fact is that, despite his almost pathological fear of being touched (and all theorists agree that sight has a tactile function), modern man has an odd urge to watch others, as long as it is through some kind of "rear window." By this I mean the proliferation of optical devices (almost all of them contained in embryo in the camera) that have been developed for the sole purpose of indulging in the contemplation of "tableaux vivants," especially if they are shocking or violent. An urge like this can only be understood if we realize that these devices and these shocks provide a morbid compensation for the triviality of everyday experience. In all things, in all situations, without ever reaching the state of complete disorganization, modern man is constantly rehearsing his jaded, prophylactic, technical mode of seeing. The invention of photography, and all the technologies of perceptual consumption that have sprung from this, would thus seem to have ushered in a peculiar way of looking at things, for which they are no more than a mechanical prosthesis. I mean not only a way of looking that can simultaneously combine seeing with not seeing, as I said earlier, but one that can experience others' suffering without being penetrated by it, as a "spectacle." A way of looking that, as Jünger notes in his essay on suffering, would find it completely natural to exercise its invulnerability, its cruelty even, by conferring upon everything real, and most particularly the experience of suffering, the character of a communicable object or "document" that can then release the looker from any obligation to respond.[2] In this way, looking shocks without disorganizing and, what is worse, is depoliticized, if we can call "political" only that onlooker who, faced with others' tribulations, does not avoid the feeling of moral wrongness which he ought necessarily to feel but instead channels it into an active response. Those who relied, and relied enthusiastically, on "documentary photography" as a political practice throughout the twentieth century may well feel let down now for this very reason. It has become a law of modernity that sooner or later the revolutionary possibilities of technical innovations come to nothing, leaving behind them only a dark pool of oppressive sadness. Shortly before her death, Susan Sontag, an acute thinker about photography, had to acknowledge it: a Robert Capa photo like "Death of a Republican Soldier" is of no more importance now, although it was once, than an advertisement for a hair care product.[3] In today's media landscape, nobody would really be able to tell the difference. This deficit of attention and feeling cannot, however, be put down solely to the surfeit of shocking images, which ultimately could even have the effect of showing up all conflicts and injustices in their true light; rather, it is the result of their total monopolization and indiscriminate multiplication and dissemination by the media, in which conscience, disfigured perhaps irreversibly, is only actualized in its documentary and acquisitive guise.

A way of looking that engages all the intellectual and imaginative capacities, the whole body, all the passions of an individual, we call, conversely, *attentive*, in both the senses that this adjective combines. "Attentiveness," said Malebranche, "is the natural prayer of the soul." From this, I believe, springs the *devoutness* which characterizes Alfredo Jaar's photographic works. This devoutness is the result not only of his profound and particular sensitivity or vulnerability to these "zones of suffering" that have become invisible or meaningless to today's political and media culture, but also of the whole effort to *ritualize the regard* that is inherent in his work as an artist. His spare, rigorous installations or stagings (so-called "photo installations") seek not only to restore the ability to look to the contemporary viewer's inattentive or jaded eye, but also to bridge the inevitable divide between the photographic eye of the artist and the acute, almost inexpressible emotions that the unmediated experience of its object necessarily arouses. The effectiveness of Jaar's work in this respect comes, I believe, from an operation that I would call "visual-poetic," because it is inseparable from a verbal operation, as spare as the visual one, but just as intense (we might connect it back to Ungaretti's poetry and to minimalism). This verbal operation not only provides an anchoring point, like the photo-texts of newspapers or advertising; it provides a story, a narrative, a *context*, capable of bringing into the present (in verbal time, the original real time now being irrecoverably lost) the event fixed by the camera, which can thus be incorporated, as a historical event and as an outrage, into the texture of the viewer's experience, and thus into his social and political memory. The attentiveness that Jaar's works demand from the viewer is thus supported by a perception that is visually and poetically reoriented in the direction of affective intensity and memory.

In this exhibition, The Silence of Nduwayezu (1997) may be the work that illustrates these operations best, because as well as performing them it mobilizes an acute and urgent reflection on the trivialization or affective shallowness of images of suffering in the media landscape of our times.

As happens, according to Stoichita, with many modern artworks,[4] *The Silence of Nduwayezu* actually takes the act of looking for its subject-matter, lays bare its workings; but it does so in a way that strongly engages the viewer's body and emotions, even before it engages his intellect or imagination, through a movement of subjective appropriation and disappropriation. In this movement, the viewer's own gaze has to be able to mingle with that of the person portrayed, thus creating a relational intimacy which forces the former to respond *by putting himself in the other's place.* A marvelous notion, "putting oneself in the other's place" comes as close as any phrase could to summing up *The Silence of Nduwayezu*, the thirteenth of the twenty works in the Rwanda project (1994-2000), as it is known, which is wholly dedicated to the "visualization"[5] of the effects of the terrible genocide that took place in that African nation in the early 1990s. In 1994, an ethnic cleansing operation conducted by the Hutu majority against the Tutsi minority claimed more than a million victims in the space of one hundred days. It was greeted with indifference or ignorance, or even surreptitiously abetted, by the media and the international political community.

At the end of a dark corridor, in the middle of a room whose light distribution is that of a photographic laboratory but is sometimes reminiscent of a mausoleum or some other type of funeral construction, the artist has installed a large light table on which a million slides of Nduwayezu's eyes, together with some magnifying glasses, are heaped up into a sort of mound and scattered in disorder around its base. Nduwaye-zu, as we learn from a text running right along the left-hand side of the corridor and made readable by a light source, is the name of a boy whom Jaar came across during a visit to the Rubavu refugee camp in Rwanda a month after the massacre had ended. The boy, aged five, had seen his parents hacked to death with machetes; traumatized by the shock, he had not spoken a word for weeks. Yet of all the children in that place (the text continues), only he looked straight into the camera when the artist was preparing to photograph them: his look, Jaar finally confesses, was the saddest he had ever seen; his silence, unforgettable.

Not to forget a look of suffering whose content borders on the unpresentable and the inexpressible, even when photographed or fixed by mechanical devices: this is the essential goal and the visual challenge of this prodigious photo installation of Jaar's. Its critical density, characteristic of all this artist's works, raises a number of pressing questions: (1) how can the image of this shocking experience be channeled into memory, not just personal memory, but political memory as well; in short, how can that silence be turned into an appeal? (2) again, how is it possible to bridge the affective distance between the wide-open, staring eye of the camera and the crepuscular eye of the subject portrayed? (3) harder still, how can the image of this experience be situated in the sphere of art, in a museum indeed, without becoming merely aestheticized? (4) lastly, how can all this be done without veering into any of the rhetorical strategies associated with the documentary neutrality of news bulletins or sensationalist print media, or with advertising, if we think of Toscani's work for Benetton, and even of a certain type of art, which seems to be at home with what Virilio calls the "conformism of abjection" rather than desperate to suggest some alternative to catastrophe?

According to Debra Bricker Balken,[6] the visual and poetic strategy deployed by Jaar throughout the Rwanda project is largely based on the rhetorical efficacy of ellipsis. The systematic use of this resource, especially in *Real Pictures* (1995), has enabled him, she writes, to "present the unpresentable," attested in more than 3,500 chilling images: visitors only see a verbal description, and are thus forced to imagine the pictures for themselves. With *The Silence of Nduwayezu* we have not been wholly deprived of the image, but the elliptical character of the series has been preserved by the use of other tropes and figures, such as synecdoche (the substitution of a part for the whole) and repetition, deployed alike with great acumen at both the iconic and plastic levels. In the first case, Nduwayezu's eyes are used as a proxy not only for the whole experience of his own pain, but also for that of his people and indeed all who are persecuted around the world; only in this way can it be depicted on a human scale. At the plastic level these same eyes act, in turn, as a metaphor for all the powerlessness of the artist, who uses them to attempt a recovery from his own optical traumatism (for some time, Jaar could not bear to look at the pictures he himself had taken); going further still, it might even be said that, in the media circus era, the lament conveyed by these eyes stands in for the whole "lament of the images"—images having long since been transformed into "agents of blindness."[7] As for repetition, which takes the form of mass reproduction of a single picture, it might be said that while the slides perform a mimetic or metaphorical function by standing in for the million victims of the massacre, there is actually more to it than this; in their chaotic distribution, particularly, they have another, self-critical function as a kind of periphrasis for indeterminability or inadequacy. Goya resorted to this at times in his *Disasters of War*: it suggests an imagination on the verge of capitulating before the virtual impossibility of representing the catastrophe. This difficulty, indeed, is best attested to in the work by the displacement (already seen in earlier productions like *Working* and *Blow-up*, both from 1993) of instruments or devices usually found in photographic studios or laboratories (light tables, magnifying glasses), as though we were thereby being invited to perceive and weigh up the artist's own doubts about the expressive possibilities of the medium and materials he is working with.

One could go on indefinitely with analyses of this type. Actually, they would be impossible if the photo installation or *mise en scène* did not at the same time create a ritual or recollective –even auratic– atmosphere (Jaar said of *Real Pictures* that it was "almost religious"). An atmosphere that can make jaded or indifferent viewers slow down as they move through the room and commit themselves both physically and affectively, before being impelled—if I may be allowed the wordplay—to "imagine the image" or to interpret it. All this is contributed to by the preliminary textual operation, whose economy and density give it a poetical character, in a situation of evident optical divergence (it is hard to read the text while walking at a normal pace, especially if you are eager to see what lies concealed at the end of the corridor).[8] It also contributes to the counterpoint of light and darkness, which calls up atavistic feelings (the child still within us will always fear this dialectic; the old and dying, whose number we will one day join, believe they see a light at the end of a dark tunnel), producing a disturbing effect that is reinforced, perhaps, by the low hum of the generators, and especially by the movement whereby viewers are invited to bend over the table so that they can use the magnifying glasses to verify for themselves the content of the only image on offer. What they are presented with in this intimate situation is, to use a famous distinction of Barthes', what we might call the *punctum* of that image and the whole work, its most searing, disorganizing or shocking aspect. What they are presented with, in short, is an image that is antecedent to all images, the image of images and a pair of lenses with which they then have to find their way out of their blindness: the image of their own eyes in the encounter with the other's.

Contemplation of a face, according to the philosopher Emmanuel Lévinas, is the core of the ethical experience. It is then that, prior to any signification, I become vulnerable and responsible for the other, even if the other does not become so for me. This is when seeing is also observing. Before meaning enters in (for meaning requires a whole series of micro-memories and a wealth of semiotic systems), looking at a face, especially into the eyes, is really an act of "devotion" and responsibility, an *observare* and not simply a *spectare*, [9] an act to which I commit attention and passion and thereby recognize myself in relation to the other, disappropriating myself, unjaded. I said earlier that "putting oneself in the other's place" summed up what this work was about, but the same is true of another in the series, *The Eyes of Gutete Emerita* (1996). The second version of this work sought to intensify the experience yet further by presenting viewers not with an image of the eyes of the suffering young woman of that name, but with a mirror in the form of a viewfinder, so that they might contemplate their own. Alfredo Jaar adamantly refuses to separate aesthetics from ethics, and these works are an active exposition of his reasons—whence their meta-discursive and emblematic character.

The experience of the face, suffering or otherwise, is a central element in *The Silence of Nduwayezu* and in a number of Jaar's other works (*Frame of Mind*, 1987; *Out of Bal-*

ance, 1989; *The Booth*, 1989; *Two or Three Things I Imagine About Them*, 1992; *A Hundred Times Nguyen*, 1994, to name just a few). What we see also looks at us, appeals to us. The balanced visual and informational context it appears in leaves a palpable trace in us: it creates aptitudes for attentiveness, or de-automates our perception and, ideally (and this is the intention), forces us to translate this perception into an active response. This is why Jaar's art, as well as being ethically and symbolically powerful, has a strong political effect. To commit viewers to devotion, that is, to *attentiveness*, but also to *com-passion* (in the sense of responsible empathy) capable of generating an active response outside the museum as well as in it, all this in a visual context conducive only to an objectifying, jaded outlook: this may well be the only truly political task for art in our days. Oriented as never before towards the most traumatic aspects of the real, what this visual politics demands of art above all, if it is to avoid becoming "pitiless," is that it should not consent, as Virilio puts it, [10] to the "ostensible" and "conformist" presentation of horror (we need only think of the *Sensation* exhibition) as a substitute for its aesthetic "demonstration." It is not enough to register the hostility of the world, it is necessary to indict it and to let it be known—let it be seen—that devotion is not so much an allegiance to what is beyond us, as a virtue of justice.

[1] The expression is taken from David Le Breton's *Les passions ordinaires*, Paris, Armand Colin/Masson, 1998. I am indebted to that essay for a number of the ideas put forward here.

[2] Cf. Ernst Jünger, "Uber den Schmerz," (1934), in *Samtliche Werke*, vol. 7, Stuttgart, Klett-Cotta, 1980. Jünger, who notes in this 1934 essay that it was during the First World War that photography was first used to record the experience of suffering, defines this device as "the discipline of the merciless eye," a formulation that is particularly pertinent to what I have to say further on and, by way of contrast, to what we might term "the discipline of the devout eye" that is Alfredo Jaar's.

[3] Cf. Susan Sontag, *Regarding the Pain of Others*, New York, Farrar, Straus and Giroux, 2002.

[4] Victor Stoichita, *Ver y no ver*, Barcelona, Siruela, 2005.

[5] What is meant here by "visualization" is an artistic operation which, while sharing a common basis of information with the media, not only maintains a rigorous balance between information and spectacle, which the media does not, but also follows exactly the opposite procedure, to use Jaar's own brilliant formulation: "If the media and their images fill us with an illusion of presence, which later leaves us with a sense of absence, why not try the opposite? That is, offer an absence that could perhaps provoke a presence." Alfredo Jaar, in Ruben Gallo, "Representation of Violence, Violence of Representation," *Trans*, no. 3/4 (1997), p.59.

[6] Cf. Debra Bricker Balken, "Alfredo Jaar: Lament of the Images," in *Alfredo Jaar: Lament of the Images*, exh. cat., Cambridge, Massachusetts, List Visual Arts Center, MIT, 1999.

[7] The expression is taken from Rodrigo Zúñiga, "Alfredo Jaar: visualidad y expropiación de la ceguera," *Vértebra*, no. 9 (2004), pp.78-91. I would like to acknowledge my debt to this penetrating essay.

[8] Concerning this type of divergence (*descalce*) in Jaar's work, cf. Adriana Valdés, "Alfredo Jaar: imágenes entre culturas," in *Composición de lugar*, Santiago, Chile, Universitaria, 1995, p.94-95.

[9] While *spectare*, the Latin root of "spectator," refers to a passive visual act, that of someone who "looks at" a spectacle, art exhibition or play without being altered by it, *observare*, the root of "observer," refers to a way of looking that also shapes the action of the person doing it. "Looking at," in this case, is also "consenting to" imposed or self-imposed rules or codes. Cf. Jonathan Crary, *Techniques of the Observer*, Massachusetts, MIT Press, 1990.

[10] Cf. Paul Virilio, "A Pitiless Art," in *Art and Fear*, London, Continuum International Publishing Group, 2004.

Lament of the Images 2002

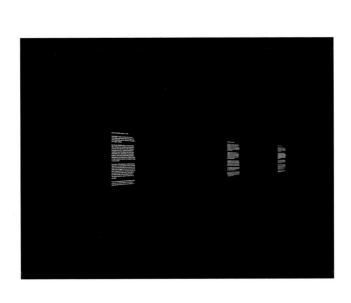

Cape Town, South Africa, February 11, 1990.

Nelson Mandela is released from prison, after 28 years of
brutal treatment by the apartheid regime. The images of his
release, broadcast live around the world, show a man squinting
into the light as if blinded.

More than half of Mandela's sentence was spent on Robben
Island, a windswept rock surrounded by the treacherous seas
of the Cape of Good Hope. Only seven miles off Cape Town,
the island had been used as a maximum security prison for
"non-white" men since 1959. Mandela's fellow inmates there
included Walter Sisulu, Ahmed Kathrada, and Govan Mbeki,
the father of current South African President Thabo Mbeki.
Mandela later said that Robben Island was "intended to cripple
us so that we should never again have the strength and courage
to pursue our ideals."

In the summer of 1964, Mandela and his fellow inmates in the
isolation block were chained together and taken to a limestone
quarry in the center of the island, where they were put to work
breaking rocks and digging lime. The lime was used to turn the
island's roads white. At the end of each day, the black men had
themselves turned white with limedust. As they worked, the
lime reflected the glare of the sun, blinding the prisoners.
Their repeated requests for sunglasses to protect their eyes
were denied.

There are no photographs that show Nelson Mandela weeping
on the day he was released from prison. It is said that the
blinding light from the lime had taken away his ability to cry.

Pennsylvania, U.S.A., April 15, 2001.

It is reported that one of the largest collections of historical photographs in the world is about to be buried in an old limestone mine forever. The mine, located in a remote area of western Pennsylvania, was turned into a corporate bomb shelter in the 1950s and is now known as the Iron Mountain National Underground Storage site.

The Bettmann and United Press International archive, comprising an estimated 17 million images, was purchased in 1995 by Microsoft chairman Bill Gates. Now Gates' private company Corbis will move the images from New York City to the mine and bury them 220 feet below the surface in a subzero, low-humidity storage vault.

It is thought that the move will preserve the images, but also make them totally inaccessible. In their place, Gates plans to sell digital scans of the images. In the past six years, 225,000 images, or less than 2 percent of them, have been scanned. At that rate, it would take 453 years to digitize the entire archive.

The collection includes images of the Wright Brothers in flight, JFK Jr. saluting his father's coffin, important images from the Vietnam War, and Nelson Mandela in prison.

Gates also owns two other photo agencies and has secured the digital reproduction rights to works in many of the world's art museums. At present, Gates owns the rights to show (or bury) an estimated 65 million images.

Kabul, Afghanistan, October 7, 2001.

As darkness falls over Kabul, the U.S. launches its first
airstrikes against Afghanistan, including carpet bombing from
B-52s flying at 40,000 feet, and more than 50 cruise missiles.
President Bush describes the attacks as "carefully targeted"
to avoid civilian casualties.

Just before launching the airstrikes, the U.S. Defense
Department purchased exclusive rights to all available satellite
images of Afghanistan and neighboring countries. The National
Imagery and Mapping Agency, a top-secret Defense Department
intelligence unit, entered into an exclusive contract with the
private company Space Imaging Inc. to purchase images from
their Ikonos satellite.

Although it has its own spy satellites that are ten times as
powerful as any commercial ones, the Pentagon defended its
purchase of the Ikonos images as a business decision that
"provided it with excess capacity."

The agreement also produced an effective white-out of the
operation, preventing western media from seeing the effects of
the bombing, and eliminating the possibility of independent
verification or refutation of government claims.
News organizations in the U.S. and Europe were reduced to
using archive images to accompany their reports.

The CEO of Space Imaging Inc. said, "They are buying all the
imagery that is available." There is nothing left to see.

Strategies of Visibility   Sandra Accatino

"The eye is the most autonomous of our organs. It is so because the objects of its attention are inevitably situated
on the outside. Except in a mirror, the eye never sees itself.
It is the last to shut down when the body is falling asleep.
It stays open when the body is stricken with paralysis or
dead. The eye keeps registering reality even when there
is no apparent reason for doing this, and under all circumstances. The question is: Why? And the answer is: Because
the environment is hostile."
Joseph Brodsky, *Watermark*

In the room housing *Lament of the Images*, three texts glow
upon the wall. Apart from the fairly small lettering composing each of the three luminous rectangles, the whole room
is in semi-obscurity. So the words that illuminate us as we
read them also dazzle.
The first text describes the twofold blinding of Nelson
Mandela: dazzled by the daylight in the photograph of his
release, and blinded by the glare of the sun on limestone
in the mine where he served part of his sentence. The following text tells how millions of photographic images purchased by a Bill Gates company were buried in a limestone
mine. Among the photographs mentioned in the text is one
of Mandela in prison. From the last text we learn how the
United States Defense Department purchased the rights to
all satellite imagery of the war in Afghanistan. "There is,"
it concludes, "nothing left to see."
Still dazzled by this last text, the viewer's eyes are then
drawn down a dim corridor from which a faint glow emerges.
Going down it, you suddenly find yourself in another room,
standing before a screen of brilliant white light that blinds
you for a few seconds. The feelings of insecurity and ex-

pectancy that overtake you in the semi-darkness of the corridor, and the momentary blindness when you emerge into the light, thus become an embodied metaphor for absence, inadequacy and denial, for the frailty and increasing worthlessness of images, their gradual loss of meaning, the impossibility of using them to present the reality they stand for—and our own inability to see.

Lament of the Images is thus a condensation of much of the thinking that has been present in Alfredo Jaar's projects for the past twenty years and more. At the same time, it may announce the appearance in his work of new visual metaphors, which, drawn from the welter of reality into the enclosed, protected space of art, may succeed in imbuing that same reality with new meaning.

The use of light and darkness, the scenographic employment of space and occlusion, the hermetic ambiguity of the images: these are what constitute the visual strategy of the works that make up the project on the Rwandan genocide, a project which Jaar undertook between 1994 and 2000. Thus, for example, in *Untitled*, an installation shown in 1997, the lightboxes which Jaar had hitherto used for showing his images are scattered, turned against the floor and the wall. The only thing that shines in the room are dim chinks of light. Everything else, once again, is blind and mute in the darkness.

Untitled, like *Lament of the Images*, can be understood as a corollary of *Real Pictures* (1995), one of the first works Jaar produced from the experience of Rwanda and the photographs he took there. Shown in different versions on more than fifteen occasions, *Real Pictures* comprises a total of 550 photographic positives reproducing a selection of sixty images from the refugee camps, the places where the massacres were carried out, and the ruined cities. In *Real Pictures*, each of the images was placed in a black linen photographic box whose lid was printed with a white silk-screened description of the image it contained, giving the date, the names of the people and places depicted, and the circumstances in which the photograph was taken. The boxes were then stacked up or scattered around the floor, with only the description showing. In the silence of the gallery and the museum, wrote David Levi Strauss, the visitor "wanders among these dark monuments as if through a graveyard, reading epitaphs."[1]

By replacing the spectacle of tragedy—the brutal, overwhelming images published by the press—with personal, private, everyday stories and testimonies, the shrouded photographs of *Real Pictures* are turned back into a "means of remembrance," a monumentum that gives victims and survivors their individuality back and ensures that they remain in our memory as real, authentic pictures.

For this reason, both *Real Pictures* and *Lament of the Images* can also be seen as remnants, relics or ruins of the shifting relationship we now have with the photographic image. This is partly because of the way the pictures have been supplanted by their descriptions, but mainly because of the particular emphasis laid on the texts composing these, on the expectations the photographic images might arouse, on the reliance we might place on them as evidence and testimony and, at the same time, on their frail, fleeting, artificial and constructed character. This characteristic, which is the organizing force behind *Lament of the Images*, is touched upon for the first time in the text in *Real Pictures* that describes the photograph of Benjamin Musisi, the driver who accompanied Jaar on much of his journey through Rwanda.

Ntarama church, Nyamata, Rwanda, 40 kilometers south of Kigali,
Monday, August 29, 1994.

This photograph shows Benjamin Musisi, 50, crouched low in the doorway of
the church amongst scattered bodies spilling out into the daylight. 400 Tutsi men,
women, and children who had come here seeking refuge were slaughtered during
the Sunday mass.
Benjamin looks directly into the camera, as if recording what the camera saw.
He asked to be photographed amongst the dead. He wanted to prove to his friends
in Kampala, Uganda that the atrocities were real and that he had seen the aftermath.

The value that Benjamin Musisi ascribes to the photographic record as incontrovertible evidence, as truth, the
illusion of an exact correspondence between what one sees
and the pictures that come out of the camera, are given a
counterpoint in the concealment of the photographs in *Real
Pictures*, the total loss of visual information, that makes it
still more urgent to return to personal experience when con-
structing an image of the tragedy. In the empty, noiseless
spaces of the gallery, the museum, memory, the absence of
the photographs challenges the viewer to trust, as though
in an act of faith, the written word.
In *Lament of the Images*, Jaar deepens the evocativeness of
these restrained descriptions of missing images by inducing
the viewer to identify and engage with them. Reading the
three texts that make up the work, the visitor discovers and
reconstructs relationships of meaning that are simultaneously peripheral and essential, between situations as different as Mandela's imprisonment and subsequent release, the
acquisition of photographs by Bill Gates, and the invisibility
of the pictures of the Kabul bombardment.
There is a subtle interplay of repetition and prolongation,
so that words and actions which would be trivial in other
contexts become vitally important here: they shimmer in

our memory as the words do in our eyes. It is limestone that blinds Mandela on Robben Island, and it is limestone in a mine in western Pennsylvania that encloses millions of images which might never be seen again. While in Cape Town the excess of light dazzles Mandela on the day of his release, Afghanistan is in darkness when the flash of the bombs marks the beginning of the U.S. occupation. The image of a prison island is extended to other forbidden, impregnable places: a remote mine 220 feet deep, a top secret Defense Department intelligence unit. Just as millions of photographs have been protected and preserved in a bomb shelter in the United States (including pictures of the Vietnam war), millions of people were exposed to that country's bombs and missiles during the Afghanistan war. The whiteness of the stone that protects and conceals Bill Gates's photographic archives, the lime dust that has turned black men white in their prison by the end of the day, and the operation carried out by the United States over Kabul, with its "carefully targeted" air strikes and its effective media white-out—the effect is that this color, this word, come to stand for concealment, violence and usurpation. And we too, finally, standing before the screen, squint against the white glare, blinded like Mandela, seeing nothing, because there is no image left for us to see here either.

In *Lament of the Images*, the fine web of relationships between each of the texts, and between what the viewer reads and then experiences, engages and compels our intelligence but also, subtly, our sensibility: we seem to find in the upheavals of history, in its events, an unexpected coherence that challenges us to involve and identify ourselves. In the exhibition space, the narrative structure which sustains and connects these accounts takes the form of a journey that is physical as well as mental, forcing us as viewers to relinquish our static state and use our own movements to comprehend and construct the intelligibility of the story and the meaning of the work we are seeing. In earlier works, too, such as *Out of Balance* (1989) and *Untitled (water)* (1990), the use of marginal areas in the exhibition venues, the alteration of architectural plans, the fragmentation, alteration and inversion of images, and the use of mirrors and reflecting surfaces all, in their different ways, served to intensify the momentary presence of the spectator, who was forced to acknowledge that the different images constructed from the various possible points of view were always incomplete, fragmentary, inadequate, elusive.

Mirrors, which appear in a number of works including *Untitled (water)* and *Infinite Cell* (2004), and light, which forms part of such works as *Out of Balance* and *Lament of the Images*, are resources whose conventional use is to improve the clarity and visibility of objects, but which Jaar employs for the opposite purpose, to conceal, to obstruct, or to baffle the onlooker. In *Untitled (water)*, the mirror surfaces do not reflect the images in their entirety but rather our partial, uncertain perception of those who appear in them—Vietnamese immigrants or, in other similar works, Mexican or Haitian immigrants, miners in the north-eastern Amazon, abandoned children, refugees, corpses—or reproduce only emptiness and absence, as in *Infinite Cell*. Light, again, which isolates the figures of the gold prospectors in *Out of Balance*, cancels out and erases the landscape they have made for themselves in the shifting, uncertain setting of Serra Pelada. Thus, too, the only thing revealed by the light cast from the screen in *Lament of the Images* is the suppression and concealment of every record.

The mirrors, which reflect back not an image but rather the impossibility of reconstituting the image in its entirety, and the light, whose effect here is not to illuminate but to dazzle and conceal, may therefore signify not the appearance of people and events, but the risk of a still more complete disappearance. Or it may be that the viewer, confronted with these works like a dazzled, blinded witness to a vision, is required to construct and create a narrative that involves a relative nonvisibility, a story that moves like an intuition about what the import of all this may be. In either case, by highlighting the omissions, the inaccuracies and neglect, the unbridgeable gap between what is there to be seen and what is ultimately visible, Jaar's works shock the viewer's anesthetized outlook, engaging us with everything that, in this process, enters and leaves our field of vision.

The contraposition between zones of darkness and light, the use of water or mirrors on the floor or walls, also create a feeling of instability that influences the way we traverse the exhibition space, compelling us to adjust our senses, making our movements slow and cautious. Just as the subjects of Jaar's works have suffered harm and neglect, the artworks make the viewer vulnerable and, in doing so, restore time to the events, people and things depicted—the time they need to be seen. Perhaps the original scene can never be reconstructed, people and events may always appear veiled, divided, deferred, hidden, but the mental picture that we as viewers are challenged to create out of our own experience can transform the works, and the happenings and individuals they contain, into definitive and lasting events in our memory.

The few images that Jaar does use in his works, such as the child's eyes in *The Silence of Nduwayezu* (1997), the gnarled or childish hands and faces, or the intimate, private gestures of love, compassion or helplessness that appear in other projects, or again the different versions of a popular song that compose *Muxima* (2005), or the smell of coffee and tea that permeates the two installations forming *Meditation Space* (1998),[2] or the voices, sounds and pieces of music used in other works, are probably there to preserve and shield, in the midst of annihilation, sickness and poverty, a few tiny but significant manifestations of humanity, some scraps of dignity that move us and, as happened with the texts in *Real Pictures* and *Lament of the Images*, make us want to imitate what we see and to recognize ourselves in the peering eye, the seeking hand, the smiling girl, the waiting men, the woman with her back to us in a roadway.[3] Thus, in Jaar's works, art, which aspires to universality, brings others' pain, innocence, hopes and frustrations nearer to us for a moment, mingles them with our lives in the safety of the gallery or museum.

It may be worth noting here that *Lament of the Images* was shown for the first time at the eleventh Kassel Documenta, one of the most important of all artistic events and an enormous draw for artists, artworks and the public. In this epicenter of image overload, *Lament of the Images* was also a way of questioning the usefulness of these modern art bazaars and the works displayed there. Outwardly imitating and evoking a minimalist aesthetic, *Lament of the Images*, like *Real Pictures* before it, dislocates the stark self-absorption of minimalism by employing a strategy that reconciles and equates aesthetics with ethics. In other works, such as *Blow-up* (1993), paraphrasing Antonioni in the film of the same name, Jaar had reflected on the meaning of contemporary art and its powerlessness and frustration before the complexity of the real, and on the ephemeral and artificial character of images. Using two adjoining spaces as he was to do in *Lament of the Images*, in the first, faintly red-lit room of *Blow-up* Jaar installed a photographic laboratory with light tables, an enlarger and trays containing pictures whose development had been halted in mid-process. Approaching in the expectation of finding Antonioni's spare images on the clean, transparent surfaces of the laboratory, the viewer was instead confronted with a sequence of shots of a legless beggar in Bogotá falling over and then turning an agonized face to the camera.

The next room was black and lined with mirrors at either end, creating the illusion of a boundless space rather like that produced inside *Infinite Cell*. The room was equipped like a photographic studio with a tripod and camera and two light umbrellas that barely provided illumination. Then, in an effect reminiscent of the screen in *Lament of the Images*, viewers were suddenly blinded by the glare of a stroboscopic light, as though a momentary loss of sight offered an escape from the infinite, fragile and deceptive interplay of reflections and representations.

In Jaar's work, the images and references to films by Bergman, Antonioni, Godard and Tomás Gutiérrez Alea, the use of cinematographic resources and hybrid supports in the mounting of works, a cross between seductive advertising and stripped-down minimalism, are intended, I believe, for an "in" public that is, perhaps for that very reason, somewhat elusive. The allusions and quotations may be like traps set for the eye which, seeking beauty, is confronted instead with the images and events that have been purged from History. In the early nineteenth century, in one of his engravings in the *Disasters of War* series, Francisco de Goya made a rather similar use of the sublime image of the Belvedere Torso—part of a damaged first century B.C. sculpture which Winckelmann had described, at the height of the neoclassical period, as "one of the last perfect works Greek art produced before it lost its freedom"—to represent a man's mutilated and impaled corpse: whereas the Belvedere Torso was usually celebrated for using inert material to represent life in all its vigor, Goya transfigured it into a lump of dead flesh.

In an essay about his fascination with the beauty of a city, Joseph Brodsky wrote that the eye sought safety because the environment was always hostile. This explained, he said, the eye's "appetite for beauty," indeed the very existence of beauty: beauty is safe, beauty is comforting. [4] It is true that the limpid beauty attained by Jaar's works is, in this sense, a consolation for pain, iniquity and death, but it is also and primarily a bait, because it is a beauty that, like the Sirens' song, tempts us to discard our survival instinct, luring us on to where tragedy lies in wait. With this achievement, Jaar places the eye, the main tool of the aesthetic faculty, at the service of ethics—perhaps because the eye identifies not with the body it belongs to, but with the object of its contemplation.

¹ David Levi Strauss, "A Sea of Griefs is Not a Proscenium: The Rwanda Projects of Alfredo Jaar," in *Let There Be Light*, Barcelona, Actar, 1998.
² The two installations making up *Meditation Space* were created for an anthology exhibition of the Rwanda project at the Koldo Mitxelena cultural center in San Sebastián (Spain) in the fall of 1998. Whereas the other works occupied dark areas in the basements of the building, the works in *Meditation Space* were placed in two wells on to which the other rooms gave out. Each work consisted of four large black cushions placed on the floor in front of a panel several meters long. At the bottom right-hand corner of each panel was an electric air-freshener from which wafted the smell of one of Rwanda's main export products, tea and coffee. Sitting or lying on the cushions, visitors could read on the panels a phrase from E.M. Cioran's essay "Degradation through Work" (which can be found in *On the Heights of Despair*, Chicago, University of Chicago Press, 1992, trans. Ilinca Zarifopol-Johnston) written in black on a white background in a Basque translation in the case of *Meditation Space* (Coffee) and in white on a black background, in Spanish, in the case of *Meditation Space* (Tea). In the text, Cioran speaks of the contradictory feelings—sorrow, joy—that the facts of life inspire in us. "I am simultaneously happy and unhappy, exalted and depressed, overcome by both pleasure and despair in the most contradictory harmonies. I am so cheerful and yet so sad that my tears reflect at once both heaven and earth. If only for the joy of my sadness, I wish there were no death on this earth," the text ended. Matching the attitude expressed by the text, the natural light, the convivial space created by the cushions and the pleasant, familiar smells of the coffee and tea provided viewers with a counterpoint, almost an alternative, to the death, destruction and injustice presented in the exhibition's other works.
³ By showing images suffused with ordinariness, Alfredo Jaar's works are employing an old rhetorical strategy. In the early fourteenth century, Giotto sought to reach the viewers of his paintings as directly and immediately as he could by employing conventional gestures from the liturgy and the law courts, thus borrowing a body language which quickly identified the feelings expressed. Praising his painting a century later, Leon Battista Alberti wrote that the models for representing emotions were to be found in nature, in front of our eyes. "The story will move the spirits of the viewers," he wrote in book II of *De pictura*, "when the men depicted there express their emotions clearly. And since nature has determined that there can be no greater attraction than that of like things for one another, we weep with those who weep, laugh with those who laugh and suffer with those who suffer. But these movements of the spirit are made known by the movements of the body." Pliny had said much the same thing fifteen centuries before.
⁴ Joseph Brodsky, *Watermark*, New York, Farrar, Straus and Giroux, 1993.

Searching for Gramsci 2004

Infinite Cell 2004

Let One Hundred Flowers Bloom
2005

As with weeping the speechless eyes

Pablo Chiuminatto

"[...] Sighs, sorrow's mute reliquiae,
are an utterance the mouth too learns
as with weeping the speechless eyes."
Francisco de Quevedo

These lines of Francisco de Quevedo, in a love poem, express
an impotence analogous to that of the visual arts when they
try to deal with human suffering. [1] The problem is to express
it artistically without thematizing the unspeakable in a su-
perficial way. One of the difficulties of what is usually termed
"political art" lies in the delicate operation of showing political
realities in a different light from that of the media which,
with their "moralizing" stance, portray themselves as para-
gons of objectivity and eloquence in their treatment of reality, but succeed only in trivializing it.
The urge to represent suffering (or present it, rather) has
now moved beyond the traditional field of catharsis as an
aesthetic experience. Art has a power to create emotion and
awareness, an ability to produce a moral impact on those
who see it by turning them into witnesses of human acts.
To say that it can enlarge the viewer's critical or moral facul-
ties, however, is to risk reducing art to just one of the many
things that engage people's responsibility in modern times.
Confronted with the facts and scale of human tragedy, art
and visuality in general have the capacity to question the
circumstances of the environment that human beings have
made for themselves. The idea of the aesthetic subject
thus shares many features with that of the political subject.
Alfredo Jaar recognizes this, and his approach to reality is
to organize without reducing and to articulate without thematizing. He has the capacity to make cultural processes
visible by working with current expectations about what the
visual arts should be and setting out from a sense of ethical

consternation which he makes patent to the onlooker, to others. The aesthetic properties of his work are a consequence of political immediacy. Jaar takes art as much as life for the subject-matter of his visual devices, thus distancing himself from the imaginative tradition and insinuating "truth" into the world of the visual arts, which is thereby stripped of its special status and treated as a segment of the total spectacle of the market society.

Generally speaking, the visual arts, and Jaar's works in particular, try to elicit our comprehension by capturing the drift of a world in an aesthetic experience, a kind of critical reflection that is capable of extension to new political forms. In the visual relationship—what we perceive, the way we look at things—the political can become manifest. For this art, the intention of revealing the structure of power and politics is a condition for sharing in the human experience itself—revealing it, that is, not just from the comfortable perspective of the viewer of art, but also from that of someone who is in the process of discovering complex forms of awareness and responsibility that are the true basis for power relationships as part of culture. Consequently, the observation mechanisms that Jaar employs can be used to articulate forms which transcend the determinants of speech, thereby avoiding the kind of proselytizing reminiscence evoked by the outworn verbal devices of politico-educational rhetorics. These rhetorics culminated in the demagogic apparatus of the realisms associated with the bloody revolutions of the twentieth century (fascist and communist). There is an imperative need, then, for a new interpretation of the observation made by Antonio Gramsci (1891-1937) that "everything is political" in this world, including apathy or commiseration in the face of human tragedy.

As this new century begins—foreshadowed by so many of Jaar's works—we know of many needs, famines, catastrophes in the world. Richard Sennett identifies a very particular lack, one that is pervasive throughout the world although its determinants are neither economic nor technical. It is the lack of respect, which, "although less aggressive than an outright insult, can take an equally wounding form [...] as though there were not enough of this precious substance to go around. Like many famines, this scarcity is man-made; unlike food, respect costs nothing. Why, then, should it be in short supply?"[2]

Jaar's work has been raising a similar question for over twenty years. By articulating what is concealed behind the encoded repertory of reality, it has brought to light the kinds of famine implicit in the organization of global society. The forms that visualization takes in his work are guided by this urge to reveal—whence its critical character, since the artist succeeds in showing what is concealed by everyday life as presented to us and in "naming" (visually) what cannot be said. He not only lays bare the structure underlying the exercise of power when the foundations of the state or society are shaken; he also shows the universal constitution of the "human creation" that is horror as a consequence of the very exercise of power. Jaar exposes the tragedy produced by this maleficent work, the folds and crevices of something that does not fit into any form of imagination, because it is not imaginary in the traditional sense of the term but horrifyingly real.

But critical fervor in art means more than just saying what people do not want to hear, or showing what they do not want to see. The power of what is articulated, in this case, transcends the use of criticism as direct accusation. Today's political art has succeeded in conveying part of the unintelligibility of human horror without concerning itself only with illustrating it. To achieve this it has shifted, both formally and conceptually, towards other less traditional areas of the visual arts. Shifts of this kind that widen the field of the arts are implicit in Jaar's work. It is important to note, however, that not just the arts but also, and for more than a century, traditional disciplines and the sciences have been seeking to enlarge the traditional boundaries of their own fields, exploring new ways of identifying and measuring the effects of something that of course is not new—human tragedy.

Twenty-five years ago, Alfredo Jaar staged a series of interventions in Santiago, Chile under the general title *Studies on Happiness*. They asked a question: "Are you happy?" His work demanded more of viewers than contemplation: it compelled them to make an intellectual effort, to respond and thus increase their awareness. What Jaar was doing in these interventions necessarily called forth a comparison: happy in relation to what or whom? [3] Against the background of dictatorship in those years, this question, coming apparently out of nowhere, acquired connotations that can now be perceived with total clarity.
The circumstances in which this anthology exhibition is now being presented in Santiago are very different. It is worth asking, though, in the light of history and our own experience, what is the question it is now posing. There is no easy answer. In the case of the works belonging to *The Gramsci Trilogy*, life, prison and the tomb are being metaphorically presented. Chile and all it stands for are approached by viewers from these reference points, not by way of disembodied contemplation but from the situation of eyewitnesses. In the history of our country, these same elements have arisen, allegorically, as part of the events making up the political

life of a nation which is aware of its own tragedies, even if it sometimes lacks the words to describe them.

This exhibition offers three works from the series *The Gramsci Trilogy* (the trilogy has five components, since there is also a prologue and an epilogue). The title of *Let One Hundred Flowers Bloom*, displayed in the Galería Gabriela Mistral, is an allusion to the words used by Mao Tse Tung when he called upon intellectuals to play an active part in the Chinese revolution of the mid-twentieth century. The work consists of a metal structure containing a grid of squares in which flowering plants grow. These are subjected to opposing forces: on the one hand, a chill wind produced by industrial fans and powerful air conditioning, and on the other, steady watering and ideal light conditions. Jaar thus shows how terribly two-edged exposure to the powerful can be. By responding to Mao's appeal, intellectuals brought attention upon themselves. Their ideas were then considered too critical, and most of them were imprisoned or even sentenced to death as a result. This was part of what was called, paradoxically, the Cultural Revolution. Thus, *Let One Hundred Flowers Bloom*, like a kind of industrial hothouse, presents the dystopia of the conditions of endurance, and also the coercion implicit in the effort to put any utopia into practice. In the case of the utopia attempted in China, it reminds us that Mao was well aware of the power of ideas.

Searching for Gramsci, another work (the prologue) in the same project, presents a series of thirty-six photographs taken by Jaar in his pilgrimage to the Italian thinker's grave. They are the photographic record of a very special day, because the images and ideas that arose in the artist's mind then were to become the basis for the other works in the project. [4] As with much of his output, this series involves the

construction and arrangement of images that are not fictitious. What could be read as documentary or tourist information is taken a stage further: the real surpasses itself.
A similar observation was made by Marguerite Yourcenar
about the series of engravings of Roman views by Giovanni
Piranesi (1720-1778); the analogy is not altogether strained
if we consider that Piranesi was the creator of the most
famed of imaginary prisons, extending off indefinitely in
space—Jaar, in the same trilogy, created *Infinite Cell*. Like
Piranesi, Jaar achieves a special balance between reality
and imagination, "at once visual and metaphysical, on the
life and death of forms." [5] Like Piranesi, Jaar invents nothing
in these images, but balances fiction and reality through
a lens that heightens the real world. This succession of photographs, new "views" of Rome, are not executed in black
like Piranesi's engravings. They introduce another paradoxical half-shade: the "full color" of the media in dark times.
The politics and media of our time present information
with a fictional structure: it is composed out of the realism
of power in the invisible prison of the real.
Lastly, *Infinite Cell*, in its countless reflections, represents
the constraint that curtails every movement of freedom.
We can go in and out, enjoying the game of freedom and
release. The mirrors carry our own image and the perspec-
tives project the "panopticon" of the human condition. This
is no imaginary prison, it is not part of an artist's dream in
the darkness projected from his mind, like Piranesi's series
of engravings. It makes us think of the prison term of twenty
years, four months and five days to which Gramsci was sentenced. In this case, Jaar allows us to live out the meaning of
the real in the infinite experience of coercion, as a system for
recognizing the structures of power. Piranesi dreams it and
turns it into engraving, in black and white, in his imaginary

prisons. Jaar constructs a physical device to shatter the contemplativeness which is the traditional response to art, and admits us to the confinement of that cell.

Chile, its confinement *finis terrae*, forces us to recognize the isolation created by distance. It helps us in a task of which the purely intellectual elucidation of Jaar's works in our country is only a part. It allows us, in fact, to live it.

In the face of personal tragedy viewed as a general category of the human drama, Jaar's work makes us question the narrative we construct as a society. The purpose of the question is to avoid the outcome of self-contained, stand-alone art: "To me, art is either thinking, critical; or it is decoration,"[6] says the artist. The aesthetic boundaries reimpose themselves, however, and the work creates a need for us to see and understand it using what Gramsci called the "intellectual categories" of perception or reception.

Jaar's work could be seen within the framework of a wholly international dialogue. This would keep it clear of localisms, but would also create a contradiction: if there is one thing that characterizes what he does, it is that he concerns himself with real events in their local aspect. Although the works in this exhibition were created for places other than Santiago, the fact of their being exhibited here gives rise to considerations which cannot but make us think about where we ourselves stand.

Many years earlier, analyzing the training of intellectuals, Gramsci dreamed of the global transformation that now dominates the world scene. In this context, the Italian thinker turned his mind to South America, mentioning Chile as one of the countries that had not succeeded in finding their civic footing despite a centuries-long "cultural struggle." In his judgment, after centuries of conditioning, the lay middle-class element was not at that time capable of prevailing over the tactical strength of the military and clerical establishment. [7]

Who or what is Gramsci? The picture of his tomb? The flowers at the mercy of a virtual gardener, Mao, whose rigors are weathered by a nature that survives in spite of them? Each of the elements composing the works presents us with forms of confinement inspired by Gramsci's assertion: prison, the endurance of the flowers, the remains of another, ruined Rome, and the final resting-place, the grave. The answer to the question about Gramsci is withheld, left up to the viewer. The appeal of this work of Jaar's is that its questions are not asked only about the system of art: it also asks us to confront an ethical perspective that, in the light of Gramsci, has consequences for the way we think about the figure of the intellectual. Gramsci wrote: "All men are intellectuals, we might say, but not all men have the function of intellectuals in society." [8] Thus, tombs are a tomb, graveyards a graveyard, prison that which deprives us of ourselves. Thus, we are told of the power of an awakening to a new consciousness of the human drama, in which everyone is called upon to exercise thought.

Gramsci says of the traditional place of intellectuals in society that "the whole idealist philosophy can easily be connected with this position adopted by intellectuals as a social group, and it is possible to define the expression of that social utopia whereby intellectuals believe themselves to be 'independent,' self-contained, endowed with characters of their own, etc." [9] There is an implicit complaint here: intellectuals with this outlook are not playing their vital part in the chain of respect between human beings, in relation to an ethical-aesthetic foundation of political and social awareness whose code transcends rational analysis. As Pascal wrote: "The cords which bind the respect of men to each other are in general cords of necessity; for there must be different degrees, all men wishing to rule, and not all being able to do so, but some being able [...] These cords which bind the respect of men to such and such an individual are therefore the cords of imagination."[10]

Jaar's work touches these "cords of imagination" and awakens their dormant actuality, anesthetized by hyperinformation. It is thus an invitation to a new introspection, one that is not based only on a rational response, because these works also appeal to the irrational side of human life. Beauty might be a necessary condition for the tragedy presented in these works to elicit an affective and effective response, and thus a new form of awareness, both aesthetic and political. It is for this reason, too, that the dialogue with the work takes us back to something proverbially artistic which Jaar's productions do not try to evade. Beauty has a fundamental place in his works, giving the lie to the opposition usually identified between beauty and the critical or conceptual function of art. His output is more than just a thematic moralization of the political, and it goes further than any "traditional operation," to use a Gramscian term, in revitalizing the ethical content of political criticism.

In *The Gramsci Trilogy*, as in other of Jaar's works and in many examples from the history of art, we move from the particular to the universal. Politically, we pass from the national (or local) to the international. Aesthetically, the work heightens the sense of the real by exposing certain imaginary connections that confound the viewer. Jaar is attempting an aesthetic experience for which he has to lay bare certain organizing forces underlying the presentation of events. He shows forms of tragedy, images, records, and he uses this presentation to modulate the symbolic reserve that every remnant needs to become memory and not merely a fetish that the journalistic drive can easily reduce to an archive image.

To say that everyone is an intellectual, i.e., a thinking actor, does not mean there is any such thing as a place where power is liberated from its own blindness about itself. To think we could abstract ourselves from the mechanisms of power, its supposed field of action, would be to conceive a realm beyond "consensus and coercion," the forms of political functioning described by Gramsci himself. Jaar's work allows us to understand the modern variations of art's political aspect by actualizing a new, ethical dimension of truth. Viewed from this dimension, "objective" information seems inadequate and new ways of looking are proposed, new readings proclaimed by new readers.

As an intellectual, that is, as someone with an inalienable duty to act socially, the artist takes up the old problems of existence in society and invites people to ask themselves new questions about power, the inevitable force this exercises, how we can avoid its more oppressive aspects, and how we can strengthen the different forms of participation. Chile has its own tragedy to deal with here, like all the places Jaar has worked with. This text began with a reference to Jaar's question—"Are you happy?"—from his first work, in Chile (1979-1981). Perhaps the question now is what Jaar's lucid methodology has to offer us in documenting our own tragedy; or, even more importantly, what contribution we ourselves should be making to this task of documentation. *Let One Hundred Flowers Bloom* presents us with the hazardous conditions under which intellectuals—all those who act thinkingly, by Gramsci's definition—make their contribution to society's existence. Visibility in Mao's time entailed—and perhaps it always does—the danger of exposing oneself to power and falling under its sway, be this physical or ideological. [11] Alfredo Jaar deals with this danger in different—but also difficult—conditions, those of today, when Gramsci's words and thoughts resonate without being quite what they were. Something has changed for ever. For Jaar, the struggle, the resistance, lies in his work as an artist, in the total fragility of the visual, and with a spirit much like Pasolini's as he contemplates the ashes of Gramsci in the poem of that name:

[...] But I, with the conscious heart
of one who can live only in history,
will I ever again be able to act with pure passion,
when I know our history is over? [12]

[1] Translated from Francisco de Quevedo, *Obras Completas*, Barcelona, Planeta, 1963. Poem 451, p.497.

[2] Richard Sennett, *Respect in a World of Inequality*, New York, W.W. Norton and Company, Inc., 2004.

[3] Alfredo Jaar, *Studies on Happiness*, Barcelona, ACTAR, 1999.

[4] The first photographs were taken when the artist visited the cemetery containing Gramsci's tomb. The following ones record a well-attended peace demonstration in Rome the same day. Then, moving around Rome, there are allusions to propaganda/advertising (the same word in Italian), a visit to Antonio Negri, and various pictures of dividing waters and bridges. There is a picture of a Kurdish celebration after nightfall and lastly, back at the hotel, Aimé Césaire's face on television (in the "Conversations" included in this volume, Alfredo Jaar talks about that day and its repercussions for the project).

[5] Marguerite Yourcenar, "Sous bénéfice d'inventaire," in *Yourcenar: Essais et Mémoires*, Paris, Gallimard, 1991.

[6] Radio interview, www.beethovenfm.cl/panoramas/exposiciones/122.act, by Romina de la Sotta, Santiago, Chile, 13 June 2005.

[7] Translated from Antonio Gramsci, *Gli intellettuali e l'organizzazione della cultura*, Turin, Einaudi, 1949.

[8] *Ibid.*

[9] *Ibid.*

[10] Blaise Pascal, *Pensées*, §304, New York, E.P. Dutton & Co., Inc., 1958, trans. W.F. Trotter.

[11] Leo Bersani, *Homos*, Cambridge, Massachusetts, Harvard University Press, 1996.

[12] Pier Paolo Pasolini, *Le ceneri di Gramsci* (1954), trans. S. Turner.

Muxima 2005

Rhythm in light
Rhythm in color
Rhythm in movement
Rhythm in the bloody cracks of bare feet
Rhythm on thorn nails
Yet rhythm
Rhythm

Oh painful African voices

Agostinho Neto

ANGOLA 72 FILMS presents

Muxima

Canto I

Canto II

O MAIS IMPORTANTE É
RESOLVER OS PROBLEMAS DO POVO

The most important is to resolve the problems of the people

Canto III

Canto IV

Canto V

Canto VI

Canto VII

Canto VIII

Canto IX

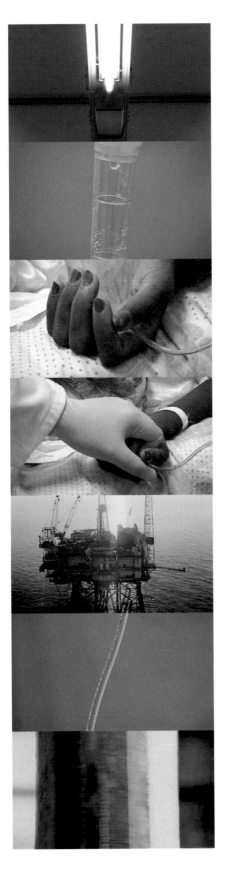

Canto X

Rhythm in the heart   Adriana Valdés

Muxima is Alfredo Jaar's newest work in this exhibition. In the context of his output, it entails what appears to be a radical change of format. For the first time, he is making a film. It is the first time his images have combined movement and sound at once. The first time viewers have had to sit (for a little over thirty minutes) in a darkened room. This is a departure from the usual situation of viewers of the arts, whose absent-minded gaze tends to linger for bare seconds on visual works. In Jaar's installations, the viewer's time—the need to stop or to go back and look again, the creation of expectations, sudden apparitions—has often been a working variable, resolved differently in each project. Here, with the cinematographic format, the artist is working with a captive audience, with viewers turned cinema-goers, with tacit assumptions, references and expectations that are different from those of his earlier work. Some of these concern, for example, narrative structure and rhythm: these become talking-points when you have seen *Muxima*.

Rhythm is introduced as a subject in the very first words that illuminate the darkness of the screen. They are by the poet and first president of Angola, Agostinho Neto: *Rhythm in light / Rhythm in color / Rhythm in movement / Rhythm in the bloody cracks of bare feet / Rhythm on torn nails / Yet rhythm / Rhythm // Oh painful African voices!*[1] Rhythm is the poetical key to *Muxima* as a work, the structure that underpins its different operations, the new instrument the cinematographic format has given the artist for exploring, once again, his African obsession. And it is, furthermore, a throb, a pulse, that comes through in the intense experience the film provides.

The presence of Africa in Alfredo Jaar's work can be traced from even before the numerous works of the Rwanda project. The continent is a *leitmotiv* of his visual thinking. It is not only the crucial impact of the genocide that has marked this African presence, or only a rational political desire to protest at intolerable realities that have long been ignored by the rest of the world. The stamp of Africa on this work is so powerful that one might even conjecture a pre-existing impression, an original sorrow, a childhood mark. Born in Chile, the artist spent most of his childhood in Fort-de-France, Martinique. The mayor there was Aimé Césaire, the poet who created one of the neologisms most often cited in cultural studies: "negritude," understood by him as a "literary phenomenon" but also as a "personal ethic," a way of moving in the direction of a hybrid culture, one that mutates and escapes—like a maroon—from the thought processes of the dominant power.[2] This then reappears in Jaar's work with an extraordinary ethical and emotional force. One might say that it is one of the thematic cores of his work, returned to again and again, from one format to another. *Muxima* deals, in a radically new format, with a deep passion that permeates Alfredo Jaar's entire *oeuvre* (incidentally, it also marks a re-encounter with another early passion, the film studies he undertook in Chile in his youth).

This format, a radically new one in the context of Alfredo Jaar's work, expands his artistic possibilities in many directions. Movement and music, and the work of editing ("fantastic," says the artist), are new means of expression, and rhythm is his discovery. Unlike installations, *Muxima*, the film, incorporates time—*tempo*—as a resource; it also incorporates the emotive charge of music, that compelling medium which can include verbal language but does not depend on it, which has layers of meaning that cannot be reduced to language or to visual imagery—a form of contact that is more embodied and materialized than sight, the most distancing of the senses.[3]

"Muxima" means "heart" in Kimbundu, one of Angola's languages, and is the name of a popular song in that country. The film, according to the artist, was conceived when he realized that he had six versions of the song in his possession: five of them are on the sound track, and the words the viewers hear (in a language not their own) are from its sung version. The extract from a poem by Agostinho Neto, translated into English, is the first thing to appear: letters of light forming themselves, shining out from an otherwise dark screen. And then, between sequences, the word "canto," as used in the terminology of poetry.

And that, as far as words go, is all. There is no narration. What we get (light, image, sound) comes without the voiceover we expect from documentaries, and this is a vital difference. In news reports and documentaries, the voiceover makes up for the discontinuity of the images by bridging over the gaps with narrative, creating an unbroken surface: we are watching things that happen to other people, and nothing is engaged but our curiosity. In this film, on the other hand, the fragmentation is not disowned. "I put these images in your world, but always in a fragmented form, so that my inability to show everything becomes part of the work,"[4] says the artist. The absence of a narrative creates a vacuum which viewers fill almost like readers of a poem: by allowing themselves to be carried away, opening up to what is offered to the senses and trusting that, by letting go, they will later arrive at a more demanding and complex interpretation, engaging both their sensibility and their intelligence.

Muxima is, as its author says, a visual poem. It therefore demands a poetic reading. Although words are used so sparingly in the film, the procedures of a verbal art, an art like poetry, are present throughout. It is structured into "cantos." It practices a rigorous economy of means, reminding us of the famous definition of poetry given by Ezra Pound, the poet of the *Cantos*: poetry is simply language charged with meaning to the utmost possible degree. In *Muxima*, it is the image that condenses the greatest possible amount in the smallest space. The artist makes us think here of the procedures of *haiku* and of Giuseppe Ungaretti, another of his favorite poets. And, to bring in an idea that is important to *Muxima* and to the art of the cinema, we might also recall Antonio Machado and his definition of poetry: "language in time," in time and in *tempo*, that is, in rhythm. This visual poem, then, is cinema, images in time; and images in a rhythm that is forged between one and the next, and between the images and the different versions of the song that accompany the visual sequences.

The rhythm of the song—which is like the pulse of this work—combines with the rhythm of the image in a multifaceted relationship that draws the two together and enriches Jaar's visual work with other layers, other strata of meaning which mobilize "the origins of sound, of the lament...,"[5] both visually and for the ear. First there is the thrilling use of sound: the skilful alternation of singing and total silence, the treatment of direct sound in location shots, or of the image accompanying the sound produced—the singer on camera, the pianist toward the end. No less stirring is the re-encounter with "a rigorous, finely judged use of the light variable" which, as in earlier works of Jaar's, is employed on an "almost non-material, infraphysical level."[6] Here too, as in *Lament of the Images*, light becomes words, writing; here too, as in that work, the interplay of light and darkness is crucial. In *Muxima*, it is used as visual punctuation between the sequences, introducing a special kind of silence that contrasts with the colors of the sequences filmed; it creates a setting that frames them, highlights them, and creates a kinship with Jaar's earlier work and his constantly renewed thinking about the image.

Working with music, as Jaar does in this film, opens up his visual work to a cultural memory that is very complex, deeply rooted in bodily experience, not only optical. Movement is incorporated too: the ear anticipates the singing and the dancing, both originally collective experiences, profound expressions of cultural vitality. Even under the most adverse conditions, music does not just express marginalized cultures: it asserts their strength, and it becomes an instrument for conveying feelings and experiences that slowly, insidiously, permeate the hegemonic cultures. Within music there is a dark sensuality that is not to be hemmed in by cultural frameworks, a vital force for mixing, fusing—and altering these frameworks from within, in a continuous process of intercommunication, "hybrid and heteroglot...,"[7] that far transcends what the intellect alone can achieve.

In *Lament of the Images*, Alfredo Jaar's work brought to its culmination a lucid and unyielding criticism of the status of the visual in today's complex world. On this ascetic journey, with this ethical renunciation, visual thought seemed to have reached a frontier beyond which the attraction and seduction of images would have to be dispensed with. I venture to suggest that *Muxima* is a significant milestone on this road. It marks the incursion of another register of experience into the deep passion for Africa that permeates the artist's work. The suffering and silence of death, the immobility of the sepulcher, the erasure of the image, begin to be counteracted by the movement, the coloring, and above all the rhythm of music, the throbbing of a life that is renewed and bursts forth despite everything. No wonder, then, that music is becoming more and more important to the artist, both emotionally and intellectually,[8] and that he has found in it a new way of working with his passion for Africa. Music lies to hand as a very subtle means of approaching other cultural processes, feeling and experiencing them in a deeper, more nuanced way.

And it also offers a completely new means of moving and touching the viewer.

Muxima brings together fragments of an impossible image of Angola. Each of its "cantos" is like a separate portion—united only by desire and emotion, by pulse, by rhythm. They do not pretend to explain everything. The great narratives and the great images—I am thinking of the mildewed statues of conquerors, of the Fortaleza (canto III), and of the utopian dreams of the 1960s, expressed in remote street names (canto IV)—are seen in this work as an alien sediment, as the empty gestures of a power that no longer exists. The great open-air screen is blank, even though the film races toward it so fast that it is left literally breathless: the artist says of canto V that it is about an emergency, Angola's, of which there are no images, and to which there are no witnesses either.

Muxima, among many other things, testifies to the persistence of adversity. It shows poverty juxtaposed with the old colonialist splendor, the heritage of danger in the form of anti-personnel mines, the search for the disappeared who are not yet found, AIDS, and the paltry prospects of the poor in an extractive economy shaped for the benefit of foreigners (the new, faceless colonizers who leave no statues or street names behind). It also testifies to the persistence of a hope that is *outlandish* in both the literal and the usual sense of the word. There are the slow, solemn river journeys in which people leave their own lands in quest of a symbolic place.

And there is the strangeness, the implausibility of a hope that, despite everything, is embodied in the sanctuary of Santana, of our lady of Muxima. This might be very far from the artist's intention, but I could not help being reminded, as I thought about this hope, of something Glauber Rocha said about Latin American popular culture: "We must touch [...] the vital point of poverty which is its mysticism. This mysti-

cism is the only language which transcends the rational sche-
ma of oppression."[9] Perhaps, after seeing this work, we ought
to add that another "language" transcends it too, and that
is the language of music.

They are still flowing, despite everything: the river Cuanza,
song, the inextinguishable vitality of music, of a popular culture that has made itself the guardian of a memory "stored
in safekeeping until a means of translation can be found."[10]
The flow is interrupted by the labored breathing of a pursuit,
or the ominous natural sound of the minesweepers. As in other
works of his, Alfredo Jaar works here with precision, with clarity, and in a format that is new for him, the tension between
light and darkness, life and death, the flowing music and the
labored sounds of danger and uncertainty. It is the pulse of
Angola, felt through music, revealed visually, as a lucid, fragmentary testimony that is offered without pretense, inviting
thought. And with the throbbing rhythm of a love song.[11]

[1] "Ritmo na luz / ritmo na côr / ritmo no movimento / ritmo nas gretas sangrentas
dos pés descalços / ritmo nas unhas descarnadas / Mas ritmo / ritmo // Ó vozes
dolorosas de África!"

[2] See James Clifford, "A Politics of Neologism: Aimé Césaire," in *The Predicament
of Culture*, Twentieth-Century Ethnography, Literature, and Art, Cambridge, Massa-
chusetts/London, Harvard University Press, 1988.

[3] See Laura U. Marks, *The Skin of the Film: Intercultural Cinema, Embodiment,
and the Senses*, Durham/London, Duke University Press, 2000 (especially the preface
and introduction).

[4] In the "Conversations" of the present volume.

[5] The words are Vicenç Altaió's, in Alfredo Jaar, *Europa*, 1994.

[6] These words are from Rodrigo Zúñiga's essay in the present volume.

[7] Clifford, *op. cit.*

[8] Patricia C. Phillips, in Alfredo Jaar, *Muxima* (leaflet), Grand Arts, Kansas City,
Missouri, 2005.

[9] Cited by Guy Brett, "Being Drawn to an Image," in *Carnival of Perceptions: Selected
Writings on Art*, London, Institute of International Visual Arts, 2004, pp.152-153.

[10] Music makes explicit "...the cultural and economic links between peoples that
capital erases [...] rematerializing and reembodying the global movements that tran-
snational capital seeks to render virtual." Laura U. Marks, *op. cit.*, p.9.

[11] These are the words of Holland Cotter, in his *New York Times* review of March 10,
2006: "...throbs like a love song, which is what Mr. Jaar's clear-eyed film is."

Graphics 1979-2006

Rwanda

Angola

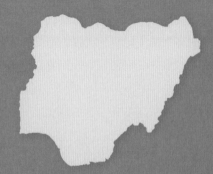

Nigeria

South Africa

Hong Kong

United States

Namibia

Congo

Burundi

North Korea

Japan

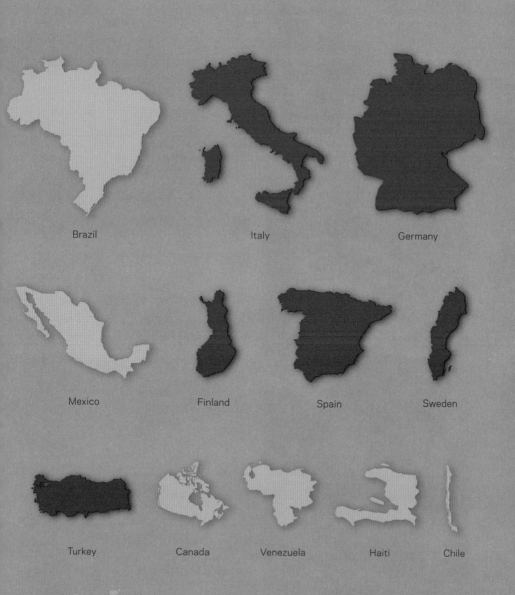

Brazil

Italy

Germany

Mexico

Finland

Spain

Sweden

Turkey

Canada

Venezuela

Haiti

Chile

Aalborg
Bern
Amsterdam
Antwerp
Barcelona
Berlin
Bruxelles
Burlington
Buenos Aires
Cadaqués
Boston
Boulder
Charlotte
Chemnitz
Canberra
Cincinnati
Cleveland
Daytona Beach
Coimbra
Dijon
Chicago
Forth Lauderdale
Frankfurt
Fukuroi
Gené
Gwangju
Hamburg
Hannover
Herblay
Houston
Helsinki
Indianapolis
Kansas City
Joha
Karlsruhe
Kassel
Leipzig
León
Malmo
Madrid
Marseille
Mexico D. F.
Monterrey
Marugame
Middletown
München
Minneapolis
New Delhi
New Orleans
Milano
New York
Niigata
Pittsburgh
Porto
Purchase
Pusan
Quebec
Raleigh
Richmond
Roslyn Harbor
Salzburg
Sa
Santa Monica
Roma
Santander
Santiago
Santo Domingo
San José
San Sebastian
Sienna
Sittard
St Louis
Sto
Tampa
Skoghall
Torino
Sydney
Vancouver
Vigo
Visby
Vitoria
Umeå
Venezia
Waterville
Wien
Williamstown
Yokohama

Atlanta

Austin
Beirut
Biarritz

Badajoz
Berkeley
Binghamton

Birmingham
Bregenz
Cahors

Bogotá
Brighton
Cambridge

Bremen

Caracas

Cape Town

Köln
Dresden

København
Dublin

Corbeil-Essonnes
Düsseldorf

Dayton
Esslingen

Glasgow
Harlem

Graz
Hartford

Greenvale
Hasselt

Hertogenbosch

sburg

Hiroshima

Humlebaek
Kalmar
Lawrence

Lake Worth

Las Palmas de Gran Canaria

Linköping

Istambul

Lyon

Linz

Lisboa

Ljubljana

Los Angeles

London

Luanda
Manchester

Nagoya

Mataró

Medford

Matsudai

Miami

Montréal

New Paltz
Oulu

Norrköping
Ontario

Oslo
Perth
Postdam

Ottawa
Philadelphia
Puebla

Paris

Rio de Janeiro

Rotterdam

Sabadell

Saskatoon
Scranton
Sevilla

ego

San Francisco

São Paulo

Seattle

olm

Stuttgart

Sunderland
Timrå
Utrecht

Tijuana

Tokyo

Washington D.C.

Windhoek

Zurich

Exhibitions around the world 1979-2006

| 1979 | 1980 | 1981 | 1982 | 1983 | 1984 | 1985 | 1986 | 1987 | 1988 | 1989 | 1990 | 1991 | 1992 |

Monographs

Solo Exhibitions

2006   Year

Group Exhibitions

| 1993 | 1994 | 1995 | 1996 | 1997 | 1998 | 1999 | 2000 | 2001 | 2002 | 2003 | 2004 | 2005 | 2006 |

Objetos, 1979
Mario Fonseca and Carlos Leppe
Santiago: Galeria Cal

Obra abierta y de registro continuo, 1981
Adriana Valdés
Santiago: Museo Nacional de Bellas Artes
Self published in Santiago

1+1+1, 1987
Tzvetan Todorov
Kassel: Documenta 8
Self published in New York

La Grande Arche
Programme Art Et Architecture, 1989
Patricia Phillips and Elisabeth Lebovici
Paris: Caisse Des Dépots et Consignations

Geography = War, 1991
W. Avon Drake, Steven S. High,
H. Ashley Kistler and Adriana Valdés
Virginia: Virginia Museum of Fine Arts

MVSEVM, 1991
Amada Cruz and Alfredo Jaar
Washington D.C.: Hirshhorn Museum
and Sculpture Garden

Two or three things I Imagine about Them, 1992
Patricia Phillips
London: Whitechapel Art Gallery

Unframed, 1993
John Clark, Madeleine Grynsztejn
and Patricia Phillips
Glasgow: Tramway

Alfredo Jaar, 1994
Jan-Erik Lundstrom
Stockholm: Fotografiska Museet
and Moderna Museet

A Hundred Times Nguyen, 1994
Alfredo Jaar
Stockholm: Fotografiska Museet
and Moderna Museet

August 29, 1994, 1997
Toronto: Little Cockroach
Press Art Metropole

Waiting, 1997
Hirokazu Mizunuma
Chiba: Chiba Museum of Art

Studies on Happiness 1979-1981, 1999
Adriana Valdés and Alfredo Jaar
Barcelona: ACTAR

Lament of the Images, 1999
Ben Okri and Debra Balken
Cambridge: MIT List Visual Arts Center

Waiting, 2000
Agostinho Neto and Alfredo Jaar
San Diego: University Art Gallery
San Diego State University

Nauman Kruger Jaar, 2001
Nicholas Serota, Eva Keller,
Peter Fisher and Hans-Michael Herzog
Zurich: Scalo

Emergency, 2005
Waberi, Dangor, Agboton, Diallo, Ata Aidoo,
Sow Fall, Krog, Emecheta, Beyala, Ram-
anantsoa, Ndongo-Bidyogo, Effa, Oyeyemi,
Vianney Rurangwa, Agualusa, Niekerk,
Couto, Isegawa, El-Saadawi, Farah, Pepetela,
Monénembo, Tadjo, Omgbá and Vera
León and Barcelona: Musac and Actar

The Fire This Time,
Public Interventions 1979-2005, 2005
Mary Jane Jacob and Nancy Princenthal
Milan: Charta

Gold in the Morning, 1986
Dore Ashton, Patricia Phillips
and Thomas Sokolowski
Venice: XLII Venice Biennale
Self published in New York

Learning to Play, 1987
Adriana Valdés
São Paulo: 19 Bienal Internacional
de São Paulo
Self published in New York

Investigations 88, 1989
Judith Tannenbaum
Philadelphia: Institute
of Contemporary Art

Alfredo Jaar, 1990
Madeleine Grynsztejn
La Jolla: La Jolla Museum
of Contemporary Art

1+1+1: Works by Alfredo Jaar, 1992
Alice Yang
New York: The New Museum
of Contemporary Art

**The Pergamon Project:
The Aesthetics of Resistance,** 1992
Frank Wagner
Berlin: DAAD and NGBK

Alfredo Jaar, 1993
Louis Grachos
Miami: Center for the Fine Arts

Alfredo Jaar, 1993
Eva Schmidt
Bremen: Gesellschaft fur Aktuelle Kunst

Europa, 1994
Vicenç Altaió
Stuttgart: Institut für Auslands-
beziehungen

The Eyes of Gutete Emerita, 1996
Alfredo Jaar
Raleigh: City Gallery
of Contemporary Art

**Let there be Light, The Rwanda Project
1994-1998,** 1998
Ben Okri, David Levi Strauss
and Vicenç Altaió
Barcelona: ACTAR
and Centre d'Art Santa Monica

It is Difficult, Ten Years, 1998
Patricia Phillips and Rick Pirro
Barcelona: ACTAR
and Centre d'Art Santa Monica

Emergencia, 2000
Agualusa, Ata Aidoo, Couto, Dangor,
Diallo, Effa, El-Saadawi, Emecheta,
Farah, Krog, Ndongo-Bidyog, Nierkerk,
Pepetela, Ramanatsoa, Sow Fall, Tadjo,
Vera, Vianney Rurangwa and Lundström
Umeå: BildMuseet

Inferno and Paradiso, 2000
R. Gallo, J. Goytisolo, A. Jaar, J. Kristeva,
J.-E. Lundström and M. af Petersens
Stockholm: Riksutställningar
Umeå: BildMuseet
Barcelona: Actar

Alfredo Jaar, 2004
Gudrum Meyer
Munich: WB Verlag

Muxima, 2005
Patricia Phillips
Kansas City: Grand Arts

Alfredo Jaar, 2005
Dobrila Denegri, Jeff Derksen
& Neil Smith, Pier Paolo Pasolini
and Gianni Vattimo
Milan: Macro and Electa

The Aesthetics of Resistance, 2006
Emanuela De Cecco, Roberto Pinto,
Annie Ratti and Gianni Vattino
Barcelona: Actar
Como: Fondazione Antonio Ratti

Works in the exhibition

A Logo for America, 1987
45 seconds computer animation
Spectacolor Sign, Times Square, New York
Commissioned by The Public Art Fund,
New York
Courtesy Daros Collection, Zurich
and the artist, New York

Out of Balance, 1989
Six lightboxes with color transparencies
Lightboxes: 20" x 98" x 7" each
Overall dimensions variable
Courtesy the artist, New York

Untitled (Water), 1990
Six double-sided lightboxes with
twelve color transparencies
30 framed mirrors
Lightboxes: 41" x 41" x 8" each
Mirrors: 12" x 12" x 2" each
Overall dimensions variable
Courtesy Musée d'Art Contemporain
de Montreal and the artist, New York

The Silence of Nduwayezu, 1997
Light table, slides, slide magnifiers
Illuminated text
Light table: 36" x 216" x 144"
Illuminated text: 1" x 200"
Overall dimensions variable
Courtesy Galeria Oliva Arauna, Madrid and
Galerie Thomas Schulte, Berlin

Lament of the Images, 2002
Three illuminated texts mounted on Plexiglas
Texts composed by David Levi Strauss
Light Screen
Overall dimensions variable
Courtesy Documenta 11, Kassel and
Galerie Lelong, New York

Searching for Gramsci, 2004
Sequence of 36 Photographs
Rome, March 20, 2004
Overall dimensions variable
Courtesy MACRO, Museo
Arte Contemporanea Roma, and
Stefania Miscetti, Rome

Infinite Cell, 2004
Iron gate, iron bars, mirrors
Overal dimensions variable
Courtesy Galleria Lia Rumma, Milan

Let One Hundred Flowers Bloom, 2005
Wood platform covered with zinc
One hundred flowers, soil
Daylight lighting system
Water irrigation system
Air conditioning system
Industrial fans
Video Projection
Overall dimensions variable
Courtesy MACRO, Museo
Arte Contemporanea Roma,
Galleria Lia Rumma, Milan, and
Stefania Miscetti, Rome

Muxima, 2005
Digital Video
Color, Sound
36 minutes
Musicians:
Beto de Almeida
Paulo de Oliveira
Os Kiezos, Producoes Teta Lando
Ngola Ritmos, Buda Musique
Ruy Mingas, Strauss
Mario Rui Silva, Night & Day
Waldemar Bastos, Luaka Bop
Courtesy Galerie Lelong, New York

Authors

Sandra Accatino
(Santiago, 1973) Studied painting at the University of Chile. She is a candidate for the Ph.D. in aesthetics and theory of art at that same university, where she also lectures on Renaissance and Baroque art in Europe. She likewise lectures at Universidad Adolfo Ibáñez and Universidad Alberto Hurtado. She is the co-author of a book, *Tentativas sobre Matta* (2002). She has published a variety of articles and essays in "Artes y Letras," the arts supplement of *El Mercurio* newspaper, and in scholarly reviews.

Pablo Chiuminatto
(Viña del Mar, 1965). Visual artist, arts graduate, MA in visual arts and candidate for the Ph.D. in aesthetics and theory of art at the University of Chile (with grant funding from the Beca Santander Universia). He has been a visiting professor at the Faculty of Arts of the University of Chile, the film course of the Universidad Católica de Chile, and two other universities, Diego Portales and Alberto Hurtado. He is a co-editor of *Vértebra*, a review dedicated to art, literature and criticism.

Bruno Cuneo
(Valparaíso, 1973) Lectures on poetics and contemporary art theory at the Instituto de Arte of the Pontificia Universidad Católica de Valparaíso, and is a candidate for the Ph.D. in aesthetics and theory of art at the University of Chile. He is the author of a book of verse, *Verano* (2005), editor of *Pensar & Poetizar*, a poetry, criticism and art theory review, and literary critic for the "Revista de Libros" supplement of *El Mercurio* newspaper. He is the author of various essays on poetry and the visual arts, and of numerous translations of poetry.

Ana María Risco
(Rancagua, 1968). Journalist, MA in theory and history of art, and candidate for the Ph.D. in aesthetics and theory of art at the University of Chile. She has written and published a variety of articles on art and literature in periodicals and is the author of a book, *Crítica situada: La escritura de Enrique Lihn sobre artes visuales*, published in 2004 by the art history and theory MA program of the University of Chile, where she lectures.

Rodrigo Zúñiga
(Santiago, 1974). Ph.D. in aesthetics and theory of art, University of Chile. Faculty member and Ph.D. professor at the Faculty of Arts of that university and also at the Pontificia Universidad Católica de Valparaíso and the Universidad Tecnológica de Chile. He has published numerous articles and essays on philosophy, Chilean and Latin American art, and contemporary aesthetics, including "Nietzsche, Comedia y Dislocación" (2003).

Adriana Valdés
(Santiago, 1943) Is the author of a book, *Composición de lugar: Escritos sobre cultura* (Santiago, Editorial Universitaria, 1996), and of numerous essays on literature and the visual arts published in Chile and abroad. Full member of the Academia Chilena de la Lengua since 1993. Has taught as a visiting professor for the Ph.D. in aesthetics and theory of art at the University of Chile, the Ph.D. in literature at the Universidad Católica de Chile, and at other universities.

Collaborators

Jorge Dalmazzo Bonet, architect
University of Chile, 1981.
Dalmazzo and Associates has completed housing projects, offices, retail interior architecture, and industrial facilities installations in both Chile and Peru.

David Abir, Sound Engineer

Mark Baumgartner, Technical Engineer

Ravi Rajan, Software Engineer

Alfredo Jaar Studio

Felipe Arturo
Vanessa Bergonzoli
Mathias Kornfeld
Cristobal Lehyt
Per Sanden
Joonyoung Suk

**Sala de Arte
Fundación Telefónica Chile**

Providencia 111
Santiago de Chile

October 19, 2006
March 4, 2007

President
Emilio Gilolmo López

Executive Director
Francisco Aylwin Oyarzún

General Coordinator
Claudia Villaseca Casanueva

Extension Coordinator
Patricia Hasbún Aravena

Architect
Alicia Müller Aguado

Graphic Design
Benito Morales Morales

**Galería
Gabriela Mistral**

Alameda 1381
Santiago de Chile

October 20, 2006
January 31, 2007

Minister of Culture
Paulina Urrutia Fernández

Vice Director
María Eliana Arntz Bustos

**Head of Artistic
Creation Department**
Andrés García Hidalgo

**Director of Galería
Gabriela Mistral**
Claudia Zaldívar Hurtado

Published by
Actar
www.actar.es

Book edited by
Adriana Valdés

Graphic Design
Ramon Prat
Lea

Production
Actar Pro, Barcelona

Printing
Ingoprint S.A.

Distribution
Actar D
Roca i Batlle 2-4
E-08023 Barcelona
Tel +34 93 417 49 93
Fax +34 93 418 67 07
office@actar-d.com
www.actar-d.com

ISBN 84-96540-48-0
DL B-37523-2006

Organization:

Collaboration:

Sponsors:

Sala de Arte Fundación Telefónica, 10 years contributing to education and culture
www.telefonicachile.cl

Gratitude

Adriana Valdés

Francisco Aylwin

Claudia Zaldivar

Sandra Accatino
Pablo Chiuminatto
Bruno Cuneo
Ana María Risco
Rodrigo Zúñiga

Neil Davidson

Jorge Dalmazzo

David Abir
Mark Baumgartner
Ravi Rajan

Ramon Prat

Oliva Arauna
Mary Sabattino

Daros Collection, Zurich
Galeria Oliva Arauna, Madrid
Galerie Lelong, New York
Galleria Lia Rumma, Milan
Galerie Thomas Schulte, Berlin
MACRO, Museo Arte Contemporanea Roma
Musée d'Art Contemporain de Montreal
Museum of Fine Arts, Houston
Public Art Fund, New York

Vicenç Altaió
Michael Corris
Danilo Echer
Okwui Enwezor
Mary Jane Jacob
Patricia Phillips
Berta Sichel

Felipe Arturo
Vanessa Bergonzoli
Cristobal Lehyt
Mathias Kornfeld
Per Sanden
Joonyoung Suk

Herminia
Bonga
Susheela Raman
Tinariwen
Ali Farka Toure
Orchestra Baobab
Anouar Bramen

Evelyne Meynard
Nicolas Jaar

ANGOLA 2005

TWENTY FIVE YEARS LATER